The Egyptian Revival

The Egyptian Revival
or
The Ever-Coming Son
in
The Light of the Tarot
By Frater Achad

1923

Preface

This little book has been written in the spirit of Suggestive Inquiry, and the writing of it has led to many illuminating ideas in regard to the Universal Tradition as disclosed by the Tarot Trumps.

Some months ago, I prepared a treatise entitled "Q. B. L. or The Bride's Reception," purporting to be a simple exposition of the Qabalistic Process and an explanation of "The Tree of Life" with its Correspondences according to the system I had studied and practiced for a number of years.

While writing it I obtained some "New" ideas which seemed to indicate the possibility of the Restoration of the Order of the "Paths" to their Original form. These ideas I put down as they came to me, and included them as an Appendix to the main body of the book.

Briefly, the nature of the suggested change was as follows: The Qabalistic Tradition of the last few centuries is that the "Ten Sephiroth", or "Numerical Emanations", were formed by the "Lightning Flash" of

Creation, while the "Twenty-two Paths" were produced by the Ascent of the "Serpent of Wisdom" from Malkuth to Kether.

The recognized Numeration of these Paths was from Number Eleven, transmitting the Influence from Kether to Chokmah, to Number Thirty-two, transmitting it from Yesod to Malkuth the Tenth and last Sephira.

I questioned this, since the Serpent is said to have *Ascended*, and suggested that the Eleventh Path should be from Malkuth to Yesod, and so on up the Tree in exactly the reverse Order.

Upon experimenting with this arrangement I discovered that although there seemed to be a decided improvement as regards the Paths below the Abyss, above it, all the symbolism became reversed and confused. Even so, there were some interesting combinations.

The main point was, however, that the new arrangement of the lower Paths suggested the possibility of a wonderful Astrological Harmony, since many of them were now united with their Planetary Rulers, etc., in the Sephiroth.

The next step was the discovery of the Symbolism of the Middle Pillar, when the Three Mother Letters of the Elements were attributed to the Three Paths which unite the Four Sephiroth which are in equilibrium. These, when placed in position, showed the Symbolism of the Universal Mercury under the form of a Caduceus and Winged Globe.

I decided, therefore, to adopt this arrangement of the Three Elements, and to try to place the Planetary and Zodiacal Signs in such positions on the Tree that the Astrological Symbolism would be perfect.

I discovered that this was possible. There was one variation, which, if adopted, disclosed some other valuable Qabalistic Symbolism in regard to "The Beginning". I explained this fully in the Appendix to Q.B.L. With my original notes left in their rough form, I published the complete book in a limited edition for Students of the Qabalah. This has met with a very good reception in all parts of the globe. I have received many encouraging letters, all of which express interest in the revised arrangement. The press reports have been favorable, and a conservative Magazine "The Occult Review" admits the importance of the discovery.

One great Authority, however, while admitting that many of the ideas are brilliant, says that he cannot accept this Reformed Order in the face of several hundred years of the old tradition, and maintains that the previous arrangement is the correct one.

While I realize that great changes in the recognized Systems of Initiation in certain Orders might be necessary if the Reformed Order of the Paths were adopted, and while recognizing the importance of the opinion of the Authority mentioned above, I still maintain that this New Arrangement is worthy of the most careful consideration and study. One would expect to find some reason for the arrangement of the Paths, and this present plan seems to me the most reasonable; in fact it suggests that there was an Absolute Reason in the Primitive Universal Tradition, though this became lost to view as time went on.

My aim is to discover the Truth insofar as that is possible to man, and to uphold what seems to me most true, until I am convinced of error; but, to change my viewpoint, if necessary, as soon as more Light is given me. If this "New" arrangement is correct, it will prove itself to be so in the minds of those who study it in an unbiased manner. In any case it is of interest as one aspect of truth, and its right place may be found in due course. It may lead the Student to other important discoveries as it has in my own case. I am convinced that the inquiry is by no means exhausted.

The Tarot Trumps, being a sort of Universal Alphabet, may of course be interpreted in a variety of ways, but I shall discuss their Symbolism when arranged upon the Paths of the Tree of Life according to the Reformed Astrological Order given in the Appendix to Q.B.L.

If by this means we obtain "More Light on the Tarot Trumps" and the Universal Tradition, which transcends what we call Light and Darkness, becomes plainer to my readers, the book will not have been written in vain.

Before discussing the matter in detail, I am giving a brief summary dealing with the earliest traditions of Mankind and their effect upon the present day, or the New Aeon, the Cycle of Aquarius, in which we are not living.

I trust that this book will lead to further Light on the very vital issues of this present Age, and perhaps to a solution of some of the most perplexing problems. At least, I hope so.

-- Frater.Achad

Chapter I
Light on the Egyptian Revival

The more than ordinary interest displayed by all classes of people in the recent discoveries connected with the opening of the Tomb of King Tutankhamen, indicates, what may be termed, an Egyptian Revival.

This, to some, may appear quite unaccountable; in fact one of the popular writers in the daily papers has questioned just why the public should suddenly show such great interest in this particular discovery, while many similar ones have created little or no stir at all.

There may be a very deep underlying reason for this, and in order, if possible, to discover the hidden causes it will be necessary for us to make a brief survey of the Egyptian Current of Thought from the earliest times to the present day.

Again, we do not find the public interest centered alone in the treasures found in the tomb of Tutankhamen, but in nearly every instance reference is made to his immediate predecessor King Amenhatep IV, or to use his more familiar title King Khu-en-Aten.

King Khu-en-Aten is reported to have been the first King to attempt the establishment of a Monotheistic Religion in Egypt, and the Worship of the Aten or Solar Disk; whereas, after his death, Tutankhamen is said to have re-established the old order and the worship of Amen-Ra in place of that of Aten, or perhaps more properly Atum.

What was the cause of this controversy, and what is its bearing on the thought of the present day?

One of the immediate effects of the public interest in these matters has been the production of a charming little book by Robert Silliman Hillyer entitled "The Coming Forth By Day". This consists in a number of Hymns translated from the Egyptian "Book of the Dead", as it was erroneously called. But the chief item of interest is the introduction, giving a brief but sympathetic outline of The Egyptian Religion, which ends as follows: "For the mystics of the world have always, under all systems, escaped beyond the externals of faith, and held close to the Presence enthroned in the inner court of the temple; the same Presence in how many different sorts of temple! The God who walked by the Nile walks also among men today; whether we call him Christ or Osiris, whether we see him betrayed by Set or Judas, he is always here, he is always betrayed.

Osiris was not the shadow cast before by the coming of Christ, nor Christ a remembrance of Osiris; they are the same, the same significance in different syllables over the earth. The machinery of religion changes, but whatever the modern man finds in his heart, that the Egyptian found also; for that is not the Christian

Religion or the Egyptian religion; it is Religion, and the rest is merely an attempt to name that which is nameless."

We can hardly imagine a statement of this sort being made in a small, popular book a few years ago. It is surely a sign of the times and of the Influence of the Ever-coming Son, the Crowned Child, Lord of the New Aeon.

But Mr. Hillyer does not go back far enough into the past to throw the most truly significant light on the present and future. In order that we may properly understand the matter, we must delve deeply into the remotest times; somewhat in the way Gerald Massey did in the "Book of Beginnings." In fact his research work is invaluable, but unfortunately far too lengthy and recondite for the popular taste.

Let us then endeavor to piece together a few of the most vital and interesting fragments, so as to obtain, if possible, a bird's-eye view of the whole matter.

The beginning of mythology with the mother and boy is universal, and still survives in the Virgin and Child of Rome. The sonship *preceding* the fatherhood represents the most ancient form of belief, and when recognized in that light, is found to explain many of the early mysteries.

The first boy and his mother were called Sut-Typhon.

Sut means "The Opener", and this may be taken in the physiological as well as the astrological sense. The Child was the *opener* in the sense of being born of the un-mated Mother. The Sun is the Opener of the Day, while Sut as the Star-god was considered the Opener of the Year with the rising of Sothis, and on his rising was the Great Bear cycle founded.

The earliest conception of the great Mother was under the form of the Hippopotamus, the Devourer of the Waters. This led to that of the Water-Dragon, Typhon. But the Great Mother was She who brought forth the Starts, thus we find Her assuming the form of the Star-Goddess, Nuit of the Heavens, who is represented by a beautiful human form arched over the earth. Her change to this human form was portrayed as "Beauty and the Beast in one Image", and from this was the ancient fable derived.

We find the Child described from the very earliest times, as of *dual type*, so that he became known as Sut-Har or Sut-Horus. Later the idea of twins arose, and these became the Gods of the Two Horizons. Sut the Opener and Horus the one who Shuts or Closes. The earliest phenomenal form of these twins was as darkness (Sut) and light (Horus).

Har or Horus as the Sun was an earlier type than Ra who later became the principal Sun-god. Har, as the son of Typhon the Great Mother, became known as the earliest of the Pharaohs and rulers of Egypt.

Primarily the word Pharaoh is derived from Har-Iu, which means the Coming Son of a two-fold nature, and of the two (Iu) houses. This, again, was Har of the Shus-en-Har or the Bar or Baal of the Heksus.

Now the rulers of the Shus were called Heks, and thus we may trace the early name of the God Hak which is a form of Harpocrates, the God of Silence, the Babe upon the Lotus; who is sometimes considered to be the twin of Horus, and concealed within him.

Har-Makhu was the Star-God of both Horizons. Sut-Har developed into the Solar Deity afterwards called Aten, or Atum. Thus we begin to see the Typhonian origin of the God Aten, and we shall learn from this something of the nature of the revival of Aten-worship under King Khu-en-Aten, the father-in-law of Tutankhamen.

But we first need some further links in our chain, and these may be supplied as follows:

As time went on there was mention of Four Suts, and the worship of the Mother Typhon and her son Sut began to fall into disrepute. A father was needed to account for the generation of all things, and gradually the idea of TUM the Old God of the Setting Sun arose, and he was said to be the Father of the Four Suts. (Thus the four Quarters were established, or perhaps the Equinoctial points and the Solstices). TUM then became known as ATUM, and the Solar Fatherhood was established. Also the twin Lion-Gods assumed the type of Sut-Horus in ATUM-RA.

The quarrel which rent the monuments arose on account of Sut-Horus (Sut as brother of the Sun) and the Egyptian Amen-Ra who was identified with the Greek Jupiter-Amen. An alliance was made between the Ammonians and the Osirians against the followers of Sut-Har, or Sutekh or Sebek, and the ancient genetrix Typhon.

The taunt flung by the Osirians at the Sut-Typhonians was "Orphan", intending to brand them as Fatherless in a religious sense because they worshipped only the Mother and the Child, who became looked upon as the Harlot and the Bastard.

This led to many unpleasant things being said on both sides, and we find a period when the followers of both forms or worship accused the others of every form of immoral practice.

We should now take up a slightly different angle of the situation. ATUM was the same as the first ADAM of the Hebrews. The Rabbis taught rightly that their typical Adam, of the same name as the monkey UDUMU, had carnal knowledge of every tame and wild beast that he could dominate, and was not satisfied until EVE was made for him.

ATUM as the Second ADAM represented the first purely Human Deity without any animal admixture. We now get a glimpse of one of the reasons for the strange half-animal half-human types found in the ancient doctrines. There is another explanation of this, however, which will be discussed later. At the same time we begin to see how it was that King Khu-en-Aten, who revived the early traditions, had many purely human figures made, quite unlike the other Egyptian Images, and that these came to light in the recent discovery of the Tomb of Tutankhamen, who preserved them.

We have made mention before of *IU*, which means Twin, or Dual being, male and female in one. As in the case of Pharaoh or Har-Iu, we again find *IU* as the root of the word Jew.

So, too, we find in Iu-Sif the origin of Joseph, of whom more anon.

We find in Unicorn, Sut the Sun and Typhon the genetrix, and how this type preceded the Bullock or Osiris.

Sebek (The Crocodile) was a form of IU-Sif, as well as Har-Makhu and Aten of the Disk, who were each the Iu of the two horizons, as Son of the Mother.

After the reign of King Apehpeh in Egypt, the religion again changed hands and there arose a "King who know not Joseph" i.e. who did not worship IU-SIF or the Coming Son.

IU, as the Genetrix, became IU-Pater or Jupiter; and IU the Son who Comes, became IU-Sus, or Jesus. The Ever Coming Son was the prototype of the Wandering Jew, originally a symbol of Eternal Youth.

If there is any historical Joseph to be found in the monuments he is AIU. He was a protégé of Amenhetep III.

This King was of the Black Aethiopian type, son of a black mother, but he married a fair wife. He was the father of Amenhatep IV, who changed his name of Khu-en-Aten, or the Adorer of Aten. Amenhatep the IV's nurse was the wife of Joseph. On account of his parentage, Amenhatep IV was probably of a Reddish type, and the Aten whose worship he adopted was the Red Disk of the Sun. He may, however, have obtained a glimpse of the Concealed Father or Sun behind the Sun, and thus recognized that in one sense the old Sut-Typhonian tradition was nearer the truth than the prevalent worship of Atum Ra, or Amen Ra. He was of course misunderstood, most people thinking he had gone back to a dark and despised tradition. I shall endeavor to show, later on, how this confusion arose.

We must remember that ATUM was born as Horus or IU, child of the Mother and afterwards developed into Atum-Ra as God the Father. Hence he became the make of the Gods and men, the Begetter who succeeded his father Ptah. ATUM means "Created Man" or ADAM.

When the human soul had come to be considered as derived from the *Essence of the Male* instead of the *Blood of the Female*, the woman was naturally said to be derived from the man, as she is in the second of the Hebrew Creations described in Genesis. A soul derived from Atum was dual in sex. The soul was divided into

Adam and Eve, the typical two sexes of the Hebrew legend.

Again it is recorded "When Horus had fulfilled the period of 2155 years with the Easter Equinox in the Sign of Aries, the birthplace passed into the Sign of Pisces, when the Ever-Coming One, the Renewer as the Eternal Child who had been brought forth as a Lion in Leo, a Beetle in Cancer, as one of the Twins in Gemini, as a calf in the Sign of the Bull, and a Lamb in the Sign of the Ram, was destined to manifest as the Fish, in the Sign of the Fishes. The rebirth of Atum-Horus, or Jesus, as the Fish IUSAAS, and the Bread of Nephthys, was astronomically dated to occur in Beth-Lechem -- the House of Bread -- about 255 B.C., at the time the Easter Equinox entered the Sign of Pisces, the house of Corn and Bread."

There had been a time when the two birthdays assigned to Horus of the Double Horizon, were allotted to the Child Horus in the Autumn, and to the Adult Horus at the Vernal Equinox; but when the Solstices were added to the Equinoxes, in the new creation of the Four Quarters established by Ptah for his Son Atum-Ra, there was a further change. The place of Birth for the Elder, the mortal Horus who was born of the Virgin Mother, now occurred in the Winter Solstice, and the place of Birth for Horus the Eternal Son was celebrated at the Vernal Equinox, with only three months between the two instead of six.

As above stated, the Entry of Horus into the Sign of Pisces occurred 255 B.C., and another period 2155 years added to this, brings us down to the year 1900 E.V. at which time Horus should astronomically be expected to appear in Aquarius. This is a purely Human Sign, the Sign of MAN, the Water-bearer or Bearer of the Waters of Life in his own person.

In the year 1904 the Law for the New Aeon was received by one of the Adepts, and the reign of Horus duly proclaimed as Ra-Hoor-Khuit.

Since then many changes have occurred on the earth, and few can fail to recognize the coming of Horus in one of his aspects as the Avenger of his Father Osiris, so plainly manifested in the great World War, and in other ways. But Harpocrates, his twin, is hidden within Him, and we may look for the Crowned Child to be born in every Heart, during the Coming Period.

I have given this brief sketch, which is not by any manner of means complete, in order to prepare the mind of the reader for the explanation of the Universal Alphabet of the Book of Thoth, or the Tarot Trumps, in relation to their proper Paths on "The Tree of Life" of the Ancient Qabalah, as reformulated in my book Q. B. L.

I shall hope to show by this means that there is a still deeper meaning under all these things, that the Universal Tradition, long lost, may be revived to our great advantage in understanding not alone the Past, but the Present Period of the History of Mankind on this Planet.

But I shall first supply those who are unfamiliar with these ideas, with "The Essence of the Practical Qabalah," and even those who have read "Q. B. L." will do well to refresh their memories by a study of the brief outline which follows.

Chapter II
The Essence of the Practical Qabalah

It is not our intention that this chapter should represent a complete exposition of the Mysteries of the Holy Qabalah, but rather to give a brief outline of some of the principal doctrines which may lead the Student to a clearer conception of the value of the Qabalistic System as a method of drawing the Infinite within.

The Plan of the Ten Sephiroth, or Numerical Emanations, forms the basis of the Work, for, by erecting upon this foundation the scaffolding of our Temple, we may learn to restore our lost Equilibrium, thus canceling out the "Pairs of Opposites" which ordinarily obsess us.

Briefly, this process may be described as follows: Prior to any manifestation, the Supreme was NOT. This being inconceivable, may yet be slightly apprehended if we consider the Air Suph or Infinite Space, followed by the potential existence of Infinite Light.

Only when we conceive this Infinite Light as concentrated upon a Central Point, does the first positive Idea arise. This Concentrated Light is called Kether-The Crown-the First Sephira. From this all else proceeds very much in the same way that Light may be broken up into the Colors of the Spectrum.

The next highest Idea is that of Wisdom, represented by Chokmah, the Second Sephira or Emanation. This is equivalent to the idea of the Logos, the Word of Creation which was in the Beginning with God and which was God. This is the great Creative Word-the Divine Fiat-and represents the Highest Intelligence of the Archetypal World.

Next, co-equal with Wisdom, is Understanding, Binah the Third Sephira, the Highest Intuition which is capable of interpreting the Word correctly and of transmitting It to the lower Spheres. This is the Creative World of the Qabalah, the Great Mother Substance, energized by the Divine Will and Life.

These Three-Light, Life, and Substance-are the Supernal Triad, One and Indivisible. For Life is the substance of Light and the Second and Third Sephiroth are but aspects of the Living Substance which is Light Itself.

Next we come to the Formative World, composed of the following Six Emanations:

Chesed or Mercy, balanced by Geburah or Severity and forming thus Two Great Pillars which support the Arch of the Trinity. These balanced Ideas are harmonized in a third, the Sixth Sephira-Tiphereth-which equilibrates them and is Itself called Beauty or

Harmony. Following this we find the triad of Victory, Netzach, the Seventh Sephira; balanced by Splendor, Hod, the Eighth Sephira; and equilibrated by the Foundation, Yesod, the Ninth Sephira.

All the above are summed up in the Material World, the Tenth Sephira which is called Malkuth or The Kingdom. This sphere is pendant to the others; it is In reality One with Kether for all proceedeth from the One and is within the One. Yet in order that we may learn to comprehend the Nature of Unity, we must first contemplate the diverse and apparently complex. The limitations of Time, Space and circumstance make this necessary to us at our present state of development.

But the ideal before us is to return to the Pure Conception of Unity, thus ridding ourselves of the Illusion of duality and accomplishing what is called The Great Work.

Had the Qabalistic Plan ended with the production of Malkuth the Kingdom or Material Universe, we should have been forced to admit that the creative process was one of degeneration. And so it Must appear to us from our limited viewpoint, until we have learned the Plan of Redemption and profited by it.

Chokmah, Wisdom or the Higher Will, is called The Father; Binah, Understanding or Intuition, represents the Great Mother; the next Six Sephiroth are centered in Tiphereth, The Son, and represent the Intellect; while Malkuth, The Kingdom or Animal Soul which perceives and feels, is called The Daughter.

The Daughter must marry the Son and so become the Mother, true mate of the Father, before all is re-absorbed into the Crown of Light. In other words, by means of Intellect we may control our animal nature and eventually Understand through Intuition, which in turn is capable of receiving the Wisdom of the Father and thus making us true representatives of God upon Earth capable of doing His Will as it is done in Heaven.

The Qabalists further postulate a series of Graded Intelligences higher than Man. These are the Celestial Intelligences, the rulers of the Sephiroth. They reflect and re-produce the Divine Ideas, and also actively transmit them for the illumination of man and the control of Nature. Thus each is in itself both active and passive.

The Human reason is also active and passive. The reason proper is the active aspect, the passive side is usually termed intuition. This intuition is capable of absorbing truth from above and below. The active reason is capable of forming a thesis, antithesis, or synthesis in regard to the truths presented to it by the intuition.

The Nature-reason is to be found in the intelligibility and order of all natural things, according to their form and the material of which they are composed.

All corporeal things may be said to have a three-fold existence. They exist as Ideas in the Mind of the Logos. Materially they exist in themselves, and Spiritually in the minds of Created Intelligences. It is important that we should grasp this three-fold idea of existence, as it makes many things clear that would otherwise be obscure to us.

If, for instance, we perceive a table, we should remember that since we are of the Order of Created Intelligences, the table exists Spiritually in us. What a table is in itself we do not know. Nor are we able to comprehend with certainty its Nature as an Idea in the Mind of the Logos.

Thus things may appear imperfect to us, while in truth they are perfect but for our limited idea of their nature.

The Great Work consists in correcting our distorted vision, thus making us capable of perceiving all things in the White Light of Truth, unrestricted by the limitations of our narrow outlook.

This may only be accomplished by our obtaining what may be termed a world-view or vision, free from distortion. The aim of all the Great Teachings is to give us such a view of the whole Creation, so that we shall be enabled to cooperate consciously in the fulfillment of the Divine Purpose.

Every Celestial Intelligence is said to be interiorly united with all things and to contain them in a spiritual manner. Thus the Great Work is to unite the Microcosm with the Macrocosm.

It is also said that every *mundane* intelligence is *capable* of taking all things into itself in a spiritual manner, and that in proportion to the extent to which this is accomplished does it become *one with them.* Here we have the key to the use of "The Tree of Life" or Qabalistic Plan of the Sephiroth and Celestial Intelligences. As we travel up the "Paths" of this "Tree" we must gradually absorb and so become One with all things in the universe in a spiritual manner. This must be accomplished by gradual steps, represented by the Grades of the Great Order. Each step taken must be fully mastered, ere we proceed to the next.

We must learn to balance and equilibrate all things as we go, for there may be no false summits in our Mystic Pyramid, nor missing spokes in the Great Wheel.

The Daughter, the nature-will, must be united to the Son, the personal-will which makes man more than mere animal, and gives him the power of choice. What is more, the Intellect-or Son-is naturally above Time and Space and is capable of *containing* time and space and all that is within time and space.

Thus, by means of Dhyana, does the Mystic transcend these limitations and becoming one with them absorbs them into himself. But the little "self" is no more, for he comprehends the nature of the Higher Self or Holy Guardian Angel. This is what is meant by the destruction of the ego; not a lessening of the conception of self but a recognition of the Nature of Self in its wider aspect.

The little self sees Nature as extremely complex; there are so many things to know that the task seems endless and impossible. The Qabalah teaches us to group all ideas according to their fundamental nature and correspondences, thus as we proceed, we are able to know *a greater and greater number of things in the light of a smaller and smaller number of ultimate ideas.* The thirty-two Paths of Wisdom enable us to classify all things in the universe in terms of thirty-two; from that we go on reducing our ultimate ideas and increasing the field they cover, until Unity is reached.

The formula of $5 = 6$ (that of the Adeptus Minor in Tiphereth) is represented by the Pentagram and the Hexagram. Man, the Microcosm is symbolized by the Pentagram composed of the Four Elements Crowned by Spirit. The Solar System is summed up in the Hexagram with its Planetary Correspondences, and this represents the Macrocosm.

Man must learn to draw the Macrocosm into himself, to absorb spiritually the Ideas represented by the Planetary and Solar Intelligences; thus may this part of the Work be accomplished. He obtains the Knowledge and Conversation of the Holy Guardian Angel or Higher Self. Beyond this, again, is the great Star Universe, wherein every man and every woman is a Star. He must absorb the Ideas of this Sphere, and at the same time recognize that every atom is a star in his own being. Thus at last will he come to Understanding, the Throne of the Great Mother.

Then will he, who is called NEMO, absorb the Wisdom of the Father, the Logos, so that in turn he may not only Understand but Will and Create according to the Divine Plan. He will then become Illumined by the One Light of the Crown upon his head; yet this, too, he must absorb so that Selflessness becometh Self and the Final stage of the Solv formula of the Great Work is accomplished. This LIGHT must then penetrate deeper and deeper into Matter till the Plan of Creation is fulfilled.

Remember these words: Things exist because God knows them. Man knows things because they exist.

And again: Man ascends from things to ideas; God descends from Ideas to things.

Thus ye have the keys of the Great Gateway in your hands.

Now it is well that we should consider once again the very essence of the Qabalistic Process and the nature of its mystery of Number as the basis of all ideas.

If we can succeed in reducing our ideas to a numerical basis, we are better able to deal with them and to bring them back to Unity.

The Ten Sephiroth give us a basis of the decimal scale for all our main Ideas, which must be grouped accordingly. The Twenty-two connecting Paths, based on the letters of the Hebrew alphabet, which is itself numerical, enable us to link these ideas and to travel from one set to another with perfect ease and certainty. The Plan of the Four Worlds, The Archetypal, The Creative, The Formative, and The Material, enables us to increase the number of things known by considering the Sephiroth and Paths as existing in all of these simultaneously, yet at the same time to classify all Elemental ideas in terms of Four. These, crowned by Spirit, make the true Microcosm, Man the Pentagram. Our main Universal Ideas are to be summed up in the Hexagram as before said. Unite the Pentagram and Hexagram and an Eleven-pointed Star give us the Key of the Aeon with its Word ABRAHADABRA as our Magick Formula. Thus we unite with the Word, the Logos, and finally with the Divine Breath which produced It.

Remember again the Qabalistic means of reducing all Words to their Numerical basis. For in Hebrew every word is also a number. Thus we may discover the Word and Number of our own being, and our place in the Creative Scheme. The correspondences between words of a similar numerical value will help us to form Galaxies of Stars, which are men and women, traveling in groups in a common direction, without friction, each in his proper orbit. Thus shall we come to comprehend the Mystery of the Starry Heaven, the Body of Our Lady Nuit. For as every atom in our bodies is itself a little solar system, so are we in the Body of the Mother of Heaven, and She is energized by the Invisible Point which is Not, yet which is the Life of All.

Remember too: The more universal ideas and reasons to which we attain, the nearer we approach to *thinking the God Thought, which is the universe itself.*

There is but One true Thought, the ultimate Thought which is All Things. Normally, that which can be thought is not true, as the Hindus tell us, for until we reach the Smooth Point all things are but relative, and so is truth.

But: The Highest Reason, which is in God and which is God, is absolutely ONE. God knows all things by One Idea, which is identical with His Being.

Chapter III
More Light on the Tarot Trumps

In the Appendix to "Q. B. L. or The Bride's Reception" I have shown the possibility of arranging the Twenty-two Trumps of the Tarot on the Paths of the Tree of Life so that the Astrological Attributions are in perfect order, and I shall now trace out the Symbolism of the Cards themselves, and attempt to show that this arrangement is the Original one, long lost in the mists of antiquity.

The Diagram of the Tree of Life, with its attributions according to this re-arrangement, forms the basis of our present study.

Kether, The Crown of Light, is called AHIH or Eheieh which means Pure Being, that which Is, prior to "existence" or the "standing out" or "coming forth" of the manifested Universe. It is also call The Concealed of the Concealed, and the Supreme and Concealed One which is therefore AMOUN. In Egyptian the hieroglyphic is two feathers, which represent AA. From this we obtain the idea of The One First and the One Last, similar to Alpha and Omega. This sign also represents the inherent idea of possible duality, or the apparent duplication of the One. But again it may be translated IU and is therefore the Root of "The Ever Coming One" of a dual nature. From this idea sprang that of IU-PATER or Jupiter as the Father, and Io, the root of Jove or Jehovah, which also symbolizes the Number Ten, or the Ten Sephiroth inherent in the Being of the One.

Kether is also called the Sphere of the Primum Mobile, the First Whirling Motion. It represents the Living Substance; being potentially both Life and Substance in the Pure form of Light.

From Kether proceed the Ideas of the Father, Mother, and Holy Spirit or Son.

The First ray produced Yod, in Chokmah, the next He in Binah, and the third Vau in Tiphereth, and from this proceeded the final He, the Daughter, in Malkuth.

On the Path from Kether to Chokmah is the Tarot Trump called "The Wheel of Fortune," the Key of Destiny which is one with the True Will, and also, some say, with Chance. This is the Card of Iu-Pater, Jupiter the Father, and it symbolizes the Great Wheel of Life; the Whirling Forces of the Primum Mobile, which resulted in a System of Revolving Orbs, the Star Universe or Sphere of the Zodiac, in Chokmah.

This Card depicts the Three Principles of Alchemy, Mercury, Sulphur, and Salt; the Three Gunas, Satva, Rajas and Tamas; the three forms of Force, Radiation, Conduction and Convection; the States of Peace, Activity, and Sloth. These are symbolized by the Sphinx, Hermanubis and Typhon upon the rim of the Wheel; while the "Centrum in Centri Trigono" is concealed within.

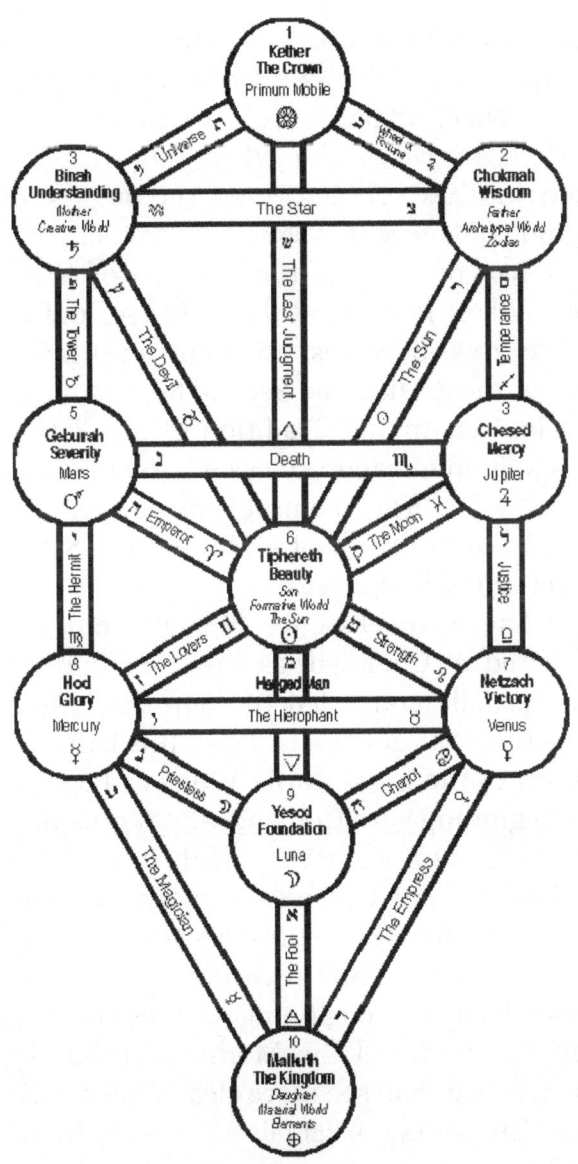

Figure XIX
The Restored Tree of Life

This Life Force is active in the One Substance, which becomes differentiated into the Four Elements as symbolized by the Four Cherubic Beasts at the

Corners or the Card. Also this is the birth of Tetragrammaton, the Word of the Elements, coming into Existence, or Becoming, as shown by the Letters Yod, He, Vau, He on the Wheel. On this we also find the letters TARO or ROTA and the suggestion of the Beginning of Law as THORA.

This Ray of Light is the Essence of Wisdom, the Higher Will or Purpose of the Universe, and as the Star Universe this becomes apparent in Chokmah, the Sphere of the Zodiac, the Second Sephira. It is the root of the Jupiter-Amoun Tradition of the Fatherhood of God as a Supreme and Concealed Force, which on that account was little comprehended by those who accepted the Tradition of a Mother and Son, with the Son preceding the Father.

This Ray is the Essence of Light, but it becomes represented in Chokmah as Grey, a mixture of colors which partially concealed the Supreme Essence, thus causing the Root of Duality. From this Path cometh the Tradition of the Light as the Word or Logos, who was in the Beginning with God and who was God.

The Path from Kether to Binah is attributed to the Trump called "The Universe" corresponding to Saturn, Kronus, or Time. This represents the early tradition of SUT, who later became identified with Set or Satan. Here we have the beginning of the Tradition of the Fatherless Child and the Mother, the Sut-Typhonian Mystery, as we shall see more clearly later on.

The Card shows a Female Figure as the Mother of All Things, but this conceals a figure of Dual-Sex, or the Idea of the Two-Sexed Son, which afterwards became the Twin Horus, and later the Two figures Sut-Horus, as Darkness and Light, and the Two Horizons. The Ellipse shows the beginning of the Time Cycle, for

Saturn or Kronus was the Devourer of his Children, the Hours. It also indicates how the Gods, the Tellers of Time, were to be born from the Elementaries or Elements, under which form the earliest ideas of the gods existed. The Card indicates the essential natures of the Four Elements in the Undifferentiated Substance from which they proceeded; or in the Womb of Time. The Four Beasts at the corners again show this clearly, and the Card itself is called "The Great One of the Night of Time." In this Path "The Light shineth in Darkness but the Darkness comprehendeth it not," for the Children of Time know not the mystery of the Here and Now.

This Card is the synthesis of the Elemental Forces; the Figure in the center directs the Positive and Negative Currents. It is attributed to Saturn and symbolizes the Influence from the Crown which resulted in the formation of the Sphere of Saturn or the Sephira Binah, the Great Mother. The early tradition connected the idea of the Great Mother with Typhon the Mother of Sut.

Binah is the Sphere of the Substance of all things, and it balances that of Chokmah wherein is concentrated the Life Force. Together they represent Living-Substance, the Father-Mother from which all proceeds.

Binah is also called The Great Sea. All is said to have been produced from Water brooded over by Spirit.

Uniting Chokmah and Binah we find the Path attributed to "The Star" and the Sign Aquarius. This Sign is Ruled by Saturn, and it will be noticed that it is connected with that Sphere. But it also represents the mystery of the Star Universe, which symbolism is derived from Chokmah.

The old G.D. Ritual (although attributing this card to the wrong Path, as in the old order) states: "This Key represents a Star with seven principal and fourteen secondary rays, altogether twenty-one, the number of the Divine Name AHIH. (Notice AHIH is the Divine Name of Kether immediately above.) In the Egyptian sense it is Sirius, the Dog-Star, the Star of Isis-Sothis. Around it are the seven planets. The nude figure is the symbol of Isis, Nepthys, and Hathoor. She is Aima, *Binah*, and Tebunah, the Great Supernal Mother Aima Elohim pouring upon Earth the Waters of Creation. In this Key she is completely unveiled. The two urns contain the influence of *Chokmah and Binah*. On the Right springs the Tree of Life, on the Left the Knowledge of Good and Evil, whereon the bird of Hermes alights, therefore the Key represents the restored world."

This symbolism is so clear according to the Restored World Plan of the Paths that it would seem to need little comment. But there is much more that might be said.

The earliest calculation of Time centered in the revolution of the Serpent round the Dog Star. The First Mother is said to have given birth to the Seven Elementaries, who became the Seven Gods or Planetary Intelligences, the tellers of Time. I may go into this aspect more fully later on.

I have purposely made no mention of the Path from Kether to Tiphereth, as this will be better understood if we first deal with those from Chokmah to Tiphereth, and from Binah to Tiphereth.

According to the Tarot Keys these are "The Sun" and "The Devil"; the twins of Light and Darkness.

The Card of "The Sun" represents the Influence of Chokmah or the Star Universe upon Tiphereth. The old G.D. description may again be quoted, but how different it appears when the card is in its proper place. "The Sun has twelve principal rays which represent the Zodiac (Chokmah), these are divided into 36 Decanates, and again into seventy-two Quinaries. Thus the Sun itself embraces the whole Creation in its rays. The Seven Hebrew Yods falling through the Air refer to the Solar Influence descending. The Two Children, standing respectively upon Water and Earth, represent the Generating influence of both, brought into action by the Rays of the Sun. They are the two inferior and passive elements, as the Sun and Air above them are the superior and active elements of Fire and Air. Furthermore these two Children resemble the Sign of Gemini."

Now, if we place the "Key" in position on its proper Path, glancing for a moment at the complete diagram of the Paths, we shall be able to draw some further conclusions.

The Sun, as a Star from the Sphere of Chokmah, is seen descending to take up his Office in Tiphereth, as the Son of the Father. The symbolism of the Sun shows the *corrected* division of Time according to the Precession of the Equinoxes, viz.: the Osirian calculation of the 365 ¼ days in the Year, instead of 365 according to the Sut-Typhonians whose calculations were made by the Dog-Star. Gerald Massey states "There is an Egyptian legend which relates how Osiris in the 365th year of his reign came from Nubia accompanied by Horus to chase the Sut-Typhonians out of Egypt. By this we may understand that the perfect Solar Year of 365 ¼ days was made to supersede the Sun and Sirius Year of 365 days. In the battle for supremacy Horus was aided by Taht, the Lord of the luni-solar reckonings."

The two Children, or Twins, represent the twin theories, and also the Horus Twins, and the Two Traditions, which resolve themselves in Tiphereth.

Also the Wall of Red with its Blue Top represents the Barrier and the Waters of Death. The Path attributed to the Key "Death" is that from Chesed to Geburah, and it crosses this Path of "The Sun." Again the Twins appear on the Path of Gemini, which runs from Tiphereth to Hod.

Rider's Pack shows a different symbolism. The Sun and Wall appear as before, but the Twins are replaced by a Child on a White Horse. This is the Crowned Child, the Son of the Sun, who has overcome Death and is the ruler of this Aeon.

Chokmah is the Root of Fire and this Card is called "The Lord of the Fire of the World" showing the Sun as representative of the Star Universe while ruling the World or Malkuth the Tenth Sephira.

This is the Path of the Tradition of Light.

We may now examine the Path from Binah to Tiphereth which is represented by "The Devil" and the Sign of Capricorn which is ruled by Saturn from whose Sphere it springs.

This Key is called "The Lord of the Gates of Matter, the Child of the Forces of Time," and it represents the Birth of Matter from the Great Sea, or Mother, the One Substance. This is the Way of the Children of Time, Saturn or Kronus. It is the Path of the Tradition of Darkness, the twin-brother of Light, of Lucifer, the Satanic Saviour who Fell from Heaven. This gave birth to the idea of the Sun as the Devil or Satan, for it represents the Sun in his material aspect, the Red Disk of Atum.

The Key shows the Twins chained by Time, while those of the "Sun" Card are Free, since they receive the influence of the Divine Will from Chokmah. The Italian Pack clearly shows The Devil standing upon the Sun, and so does Levi. This is the Card of Ayin, the Eye. It represents the Eye doctrine rather than that of the Head or Heart. The Sut-Typhonian calculation of Time was incorrect in representing the Year by 365 days.

Notice in this card there is also a Wall, but the color symbolism is reversed. This again indicates the Wall of "Death" whose path this one crosses in the same manner as that of the Sun on the opposite side of the Tree.

This Path of "The Devil" represents the Sut-Typhonian tradition of Set or Satan, as its ruler was afterwards called. The Path of "The Sun" represents the tradition of the Jupiter-Ammonians with Horus as its ruler. Horus of the Star is the reconciler between them.

Both the traditions of Light and Darkness as opposed to each other sprang from the Primal Idea of the Pure Spiritual Light of The Ever Coming Son, IU, the Holy Child of Kether. So we may now examine the Path from Kether to Tiphereth, that of the Influence of the Supreme and Concealed Father of All becoming Manifested in the Son in whom Glory and Suffering are identical.

This, by Tarot, is the Card called "Judgment" attributed to the Letter SHIN, the true Fire of the Spirit, and the progenitor of the Sun behind the Sun. This is the equilibrated Triple Flame of the Supreme Godhead, the Winged Globe of the Three Supernals, the Head of the Staff of the Universal Mercury, the Absolute Reason of All Things.

The Influence of this Path causes the Dead to rise from their tombs in the Resurrection of the pure Spirit and the Regeneration of Matter. It passes through the Path of "The Star" as the Child of Chokmah and Binah which overcomes Death. It is the Path of the Ever-living One coming into Manifestation, it represents the Absolute and Universal Tradition of the Golden Age. "It is called the Card of Perpetual Intelligence because it *regulateth* the motions of the Sun and Moon (Tiphereth and Yesod) in their proper Order, each in an orbit convenient to it" (Sepher Yetzirah).

The Paths of "The Sun" and "Devil" merely suggest man's attempts to discover the true Motions and Order of the Universe, and to translate them into Time. This Path *actually regulates these motions*, therefore suggests, perhaps, the true calculation of the Course of the whole Solar System round the invisible Center of All.

It is said in the Old G.D. Ritual: "This card is a glyph of the powers of fire. The Angel crowned with the Sun is Michael, the Ruler of the Solar Fire. The Serpents which leap in the Rainbow are symbols of the Fiery Seraphim. The Trumpet represents the influence of the Spirit descending upon Binah (this according to my opinion should be Tiphereth), the Banner and Cross refer to the rivers of Paradise."

But in this Card we are able to trace the symbolism of the Divine Breath of Kether, not whispering the Work in Chokmah, but coming to us through the Trumpet of the Sun, ever proclaiming the Brightness of the Lord and Giver of Life to all men. And this Trumpet is the Horn that is exhalted for ever. The Path combines the Mysteries of the Death and Resurrection as shown in "The Sun"; and the Erection and Re-erection of "The Devil" with the Generation and Regeneration of the Spirit.

As shown in "Q. B. L.," Shin represents the Roots of the Elements, the essences of Kether, Chokmah and Binah, concentrated in Tiphereth. It also represents "Number," the first of the Three Creative Sepharim of the Sepher Yetzirah.

Having dealt with the most direct influences descending upon Tiphereth, and we must next consider the supporting Pillars and the indirect influences through Chesed and Geburah.

Let us take the Path from Chokmah to Chesed, and then follow the one from Chesed to Tiphereth, thus completing the Right side first.

The Key to the Influence between Chokmah and Chesed is called "Temperance" and is attributed to the Sign Sagittarius. A Figure is seen pouring fluid from one urn to another. It represents "Preservation," as opposed to the "Destruction" of the Path of the "Blasted Tower" on the opposite side, while the equilibrated Path in the Center is that of "Creation" and "Regeneration" as before noticed.

Sagittarius is the Sign symbolized by the Archer who is half man, half horse. The Horse is said to be the gift to man of the Goddess of Wisdom, viz.: Chokmah. This Sign is Ruled by Jupiter and it receives the Influence of the Path of IU-PATER through Chokmah. It is also connected directly with the Sphere of Jupiter or Chesed. This gives us some indication of the dual-symbolism of the Forces of Life in the two Urns held by the figure on the Card. We may also glimpse some idea of the Ascending and Descending Arrows of the AA or

IU. Again we have the ascent and descent of the Wheel of Life or Zodiac which revolves, so to speak, as Chokmah, between the two Jupiterial influences.

The Figure is clothed in Red and Blue, for Chokmah is the "Root of Fire" and Chesed the "Sphere of Water." It stands on Water, or Chesed, but the Robe immediately above the Water is Red, for Sagittarius is a Fiery Sign.

In Rider's Pack we actually see a "Path and a Sun" to the left of the Figure, just where the Path of the Sun comes in this arrangement. The Sign of Fire is on the Breast of the Figure, above which is faintly seen the Hebrew IHVH, the Word of the Father, Chokmah.

Chesed is the Sephira of Mercy (opposed to that of Severity, Geburah) and also that of Authority for it Transmits or reflects the Word of the Father or Logos.

The Path from Chesed to Tiphereth is that of "The Moon" by Tarot and is attributed to the Sign of Pisces, which in turn is Ruled by Jupiter. Through this Path came the Piscean Tradition of the Fish-God, another aspect of Horus as the Solar Deity or Son.

The Card itself is described in the old G.D. Ritual as follows (we should place the card in position on the Tree and study the symbolism carefully):

"It represents the Moon in its increase in the side of *Gedulah* (Chesed), it has sixteen principal and sixteen secondary rays. *Four* Hebrew Yods fall from it (4 = Chesed the representative of the Law of the Father). There are two Watchtowers, Two Dogs and a Crayfish. The Four Yods represent the letters of the Holy Name (transmitted from the breast of the Figure of Temperance). The Crayfish is emblem of the Sun (Tiphereth) below the horizon, as he ever is when the Moon is increasing above."

As we shall see later the Path of the "Sun" is that of the Setting Sun. The Moon God was known as "Sin" whose word is restriction, and this has been characteristic of the Piscean Age just passed. The true tradition of the Sun became clouded in that age.

The Moon transmits some Light even if it is but a reflector of the Sun. The Word of Sin being Restriction, we may notice how the influence of "Preservation" became that of "Repression" which is but a partial understanding of the idea.

On the other hand, we should next study the Path from Binah to Geburah and then the one from Geburah to Tiphereth. These represent the opposite tradition of Over Indulgence, or "Destruction" through Waste of Life.

The Path from Binah, the Primal Mother, to Geburah the Sphere of Mars, is by Tarot "The Blasted Tower" and it is attributed to the Planet Mars. Here we see another aspect of Horus as the God of War and Vengeance.

The G.D. Ritual says: "It represents a Tower struck by a lightning flash proceeding from a rayed circle and terminating in a triangle. It is the Tower of Babel. The flash exactly forms the Astronomical Symbol of Mars. It is the power of the Triad (concentrated in Binah, 3) rushing down and destroying the Column of Darkness (the Pillar of Severity, also the Dark Tradition). The men falling from the Tower represent the fall of the Kings of Edom."

"On the *Right Hand* side of the Tower is Light and the representation of the Tree of Life by Ten Circles, on the *Left Hand* is Darkness, and eleven Circles symbolizing the Qliphoth."

Here the tradition of Light and Darkness is clearly indicated. The fall of the Tower of Babel resulted in the loss of the Universal Language, since when confusion has prevailed. The Sons of Darkness for a time retrogressed, while the followers of the Tradition of Light were advancing. This is the result of the Positive and Negative Currents from the "Path of Saturn" through Binah the Dark Sphere.

The influence of Mars, passing through Geburah, the Sphere of Mars and of Severity, is transmitted to Tiphereth by the Path of Aries, or "The Emperor." Aries is Ruled by Mars and is the House of the Exaltation of the Sun. The Ram or Lamb was sacrificed as a *substitute* for Man, so this path represents "Substitution" as that of Pisces, on the opposite side, represents "Reflection." Both are partial truths. This Path also transmits the "Personal Will" of Geburah to Tiphereth. When the Personal Will is substituted for the Divine or True Will trouble arises. In Tiphereth, The Heart, both the Personal and True Wills are harmonized, or apparently so.

Aries and Pisces are seen with the Sun, or Tiphereth, as reconciler between them, as in the beginning of the Great Cycle, with the Sun in His Natural place, unaffected by the Precession of the Equinoxes. In this position the Jupiter-Ammonian, and the Sut-Typhonian controversy is temporarily harmonized.

The Reciprocal Path from Chesed, Mercy, to Geburah, Severity, is that of "Death" the Great Transformer. The Sign Scorpio is its Yetziratic attribution, and this is Ruled by Mars the Destroyer. Death is both the enemy and the friend in one, for in truth there is no "death," but only a "Change of Life." The Card shows a Skeleton with a scythe, he is cutting down heads (one of which is crowned) but the "rise again" as soon as he passes over them, for the Influences of the Paths of "Resurrection," "Regeneration," and "Re-erection" all play upon this one. The Path of Shin, equilibrating Light and Darkness, rules over all, for this Path is that of the Influence of IU the Ever-coming Son, the true Horus whose appearance in Aries is as the Lamb, in Pisces as the Fish, or in the earlier Signs as The Lion, The Beetle, The Twins, or the Bull.

We have seen how the Influence of the Tradition of Light flows down into Tiphereth through two channels. The Paths of IU-PATER, Chokmah, and The Sun, and those of IU-PATER, Chokmah, Sagittarius, Chesed, and Pisces.

We have likewise traced the Tradition of Darkness through the Paths of Saturn, Binah and Capricorn, to Tiphereth; and also through Saturn, Binah, Mars, Geburah, and Aries, to the same Sphere.

The Universal Tradition which transcends both the Light and the Darkness, descends from Kether-Pure Being, by the Path of Shin or Spirit, through the Path of Aquarius, The Star of Hope, and that of Scorpio, Death and Despair, directly upon Tiphereth. This is the Line of Equilibrium between the Balanced Ideas of Good and Evil; Light and Darkness; Preservation and Destruction, etc. This is the Path of the Doctrine of the Heart, which unites with those of the Eye and the Head (Ayin and Resh) in Tiphereth the Sphere of the Heart, or the Son, wherein all things are Beautified and Harmonized.

It should be noticed that the Direct Influence of the Supernals upon Tiphereth comes from the Paths of Resh and Ayin uniting with those of Shin and Tzaddi.

The Numerical Value of these Letters added to Tiphereth is 200 + 70 + 300 + 90 + 6 = 666, the Grand Scale Number of The Sun, and of the Beast or Man. Again, the Descending Triad of the Sephiroth Binah, Chokmah, Tiphereth is 326 [i.e. by concatenating the numbers of those Sephiroth.-B.R.] the Numeration of IShVH the Redeemer, the formula of the Descent of Shin into IHVH or of Spirit into Matter. 326 is also the Numeration of PARChVAL in the oldest form, which became PARZIVAL who is 418 in the New Aeon; thus connecting him with ABRAHADABRA, the Word of the Aeon, and the Reward of Ra-Hoor-Khuit; as will be more fully discussed later on. For the moment we should notice that The Beast, The Word of the Aeon, and Parzival are Harmonized in Tiphereth, as are all aspects of the Sun and the Son, although there may appear to be "division hither homeward."

The Sephiroth and Paths so far taken into consideration, form the great Heavenly Hexagram, the Center of which is Spirit, although this central point is not indicated by any Sephira, but only by the Path of Shin. In the Tarot Key "The Judgment" this Invisible Breath of Spirit proceeds from the Mouth of the Trumpet in the Center of the Card.

If we examine this Hexagram, we notice that the Hebrew Letters on the Paths forming the Hexagon, are as follows: Kaph, Samek, Qoph, He, Pe, Tau: or 20+60+100+5+80+400 = 665 which is the number of BITh HRChM, meaning The Womb. This does represent The Womb of Creation, for these paths outline the Circle of the "Key of Life" or Ankh, upon which the Tree of Life is built.

We should notice also the peculiar arrangement of the Hexagram. There are four interior Paths, forming the bases of four similar Triangles. These Paths are those of "The Star," "The Sun," "Death" and "The Devil". They may be said to symbolically represent the Sun in the Four Quarters. Thus, "The Devil," although the basis of the Tradition of Darkness, represents the Rising Sun of the Eastern Horizon; for SUT is the "Opener" of the Day. This Dark Tradition gradually resulted in a Lurid Dawn. The Path of "The Sun" represents the Setting Sun, since the tradition of Light tended to become "Twilight." This is the Path of Horus, Lord of the Western Horizon, who closed the Day. Together they are Sut-Horus the Twin Lion Gods. The Path of "The Star" represents the Sun of Midday, at its height; thus "The One Star in Sight" during the Day. This position of the Sun has been called AHATHOOR, and in the Tarot Card we see that Goddess. But AHA is also a title of Horus, as is HAR and HAR-MAKHU, which means Horus of the Star. This is his Name as Opener of the Year, and it is His Influence which descends through the Path of Shin, as the Sun behind the Sun.

The Path of "Death" represents the Sun of Midnight, in the Underworld.

There came a period in Egyptian tradition when Four Suts were recognized as those of the Four Quarters, these were then called the Children of TUM, the Setting Sun, who became ATUM, and afterwards ATUM-RA, the Solar Deity as Father of All Things. This was the period when the Supreme and Concealed Father had been entirely lost to the followers of the Tradition of Light, while the Doctrine of the Mother and Child as First Cause had fallen into disrepute as representing the Tradition of Darkness. The Influence of the Supreme still descended upon Tiphereth, the Sun, through IU, but was only recognized by the few followers of the Universal Tradition of the Golden Age. All these traditions became merged in Tiphereth and there Harmonized, though the result was not an absolutely true one. An attempt to establish the truth was made by Amenhatep IV, or King Khu-en-Aten, who revived Aten Worship in place of that of Atum Ra, or Amen Ra; but he was ahead of his time, and it remained for the Present Aeon to re-establish the truth, as we shall endeavor to show more clearly further on.

We may remark, however, that the Universal Mercury is said to be "All present in Heaven and in Hell" so that we find the Ideas of Lucifer or Satan as the Sun, blended with those of the Sun of Light, and the Sun of the Universe, in the Heart of Man. Also we may notice how the Higher Will comes down to Tiphereth from Chokmah, and the lower or personal will through Geburah. These are both blended in Tiphereth, the Heart.

The "Circle" of the "Key of Life" having been formed; now follows the "Cross" which completes the Ankh. But at this point we shall notice a "Passover" or Crossing over of the dual Currents, for the "Middle Pillar" is the Caduceus, and the twin-serpents, while knotted together in Tiphereth, cross and re-unite lower down. This is symbolized clearly by the Three Mother Letters of the Elements, or the Three Sepharim of Number, Writing, and Speech; as explained in Q. B. L.

These are Shin above Mem, above Aleph. We have already dealt with Shin as IU, which it symbolizes perfectly, since if we place the "I" inside the "U," the letter Shin is formed. These are the letters of the Father and Son, who are united in Tiphereth.

Let us now trace the Currents as they "cross-over". The Influence from the Path of Aries, joining Geburah and Tiphereth, passes through the latter and emerges as a channel from Tiphereth to Netzach. This in the Tarot is the Key called "Strength" and it is attributed to the Sign Leo which is Ruled by the Sun.

The Card shows a Woman closing (or opening) the mouth of a Lion. This is clearly the Woman of Venus, or Netzach, united with the Lion of the Sun or Tiphereth. The Ram, or Lamb (another form of Horus) has been sacrificed as a substitute, and passes through the Solar Fire at the "Passover." In the City of the Sun it may truly be said that "The Lion lies down with the Lamb"; both are aspects of Horus, their paths are seen united in Tiphereth.

This Lion may be called "The Green Lion" where the Path meets Netzach (Emerald Green), and "The Red Lion" as he approaches the Sun. Again we find symbolism of the Twin Lions of Horus (as later they appear as the twin Sphinxes of the Charioteer). We see the "Strength" of Geburah, transmitted through the Ram and the Sun, to this Path, where its Animal Nature becomes subdued by the Pure Love of the Woman of Netzach. Thus the Dark tradition becomes purified through this process.

On the other hand, the Path from Chesed to Tiphereth ("The Moon" by Tarot, or Sign of Pisces) emerges from its Solar Bath, as the Path of "The Lovers" or Gemini, which unites Tiphereth with Hod. Gemini is Ruled by Mercury whose sphere is Hod. We may then trace the "Wisdom" from Chokmah, through paths of Light, as it flows into this reservoir of pure Reason, carrying with it the ideas of the "Pairs of

Opposites" from "Temperance", "The Moon" (with its twin towers), and "The Lovers" or Gemini.

This Key, "The Lovers", depicts the Symbolism perfectly. The Card shows the Sun above the heads of the Figures, just as they are relatively to Tiphereth. Beneath it are the Twins, the same Children we saw in the path of "The Sun" transmitting the Tradition from Chokmah. They have overcome the illusion of the "Moon" with its restrictions. Cupid is seen with his Bow and Arrow (perhaps the Bow of the Moon and the Arrow of Sagittarius). Sometimes this card is shown as symbolizing a Man between two Women representing Virtue and Vice (so-called). He must learn to treat them both alike, and harmonize these ideas in the Light of Tiphereth, the Heart. This was a very necessary lesson for the followers of the White Tradition to learn, for the twilight had made their view narrow and restricted, therefore an elements of Sin (the Moon God) had entered, and the earlier Wisdom had been lost.

We may now consider the Influence of the Side Pillars. On the one hand we find "Justice" or Libra which is Ruled by Venus, bringing down the Mercy of Chesed to Netzach the Sphere of Venus. Here we see the Law of Love coming into operation under the Will of Chokmah, as it is written, "Love is the law, love under will". Love needs to be Balanced in Netzach, thus avoiding extremes. Opposite to this Path is that which transmits the Strength of Geburah to the Sphere of Mercury or Hod. The Influence herein operative is that of "The Hermit" or Virgo, which is Ruled by Mercury. One must be reasonable in regard to one's Virginity, but the Power of the Virgin is great.

Herein we find the Dark Tradition transformed into a wise Reserve or Secrecy. The Hermit merely conceals the Light in his Cloak, while he carries his Staff in his hand. This represents a better adjustment of the Life, which is the Substance of Light; the excess of the Path of the "Tower" is tempered down to a wise control. This refers also to the Control of Speech; the Tower was that of Babel, and its destruction caused the confusion of tongues, while here we see a re-adjustment as this path enters the Domain of Mercury, which contains the influence from Chokmah, the "Word" lost to the Dark Brothers for a time.

Few realize the secrets of the Tradition of the Widow's son, and the Substitute, and the Lost Word, as depicted in this Left Hand side of the Tree.

Uniting the Sephiroth Netzach and Hod is the Path of "The Hierophant", the Initiator into the Mysteries of Osiris the Bull. This Path is attributed to the Sign Taurus which is Ruled by Venus or Netzach. Venus and Mercury are herein united in a Wise and Initiated Love of a reciprocal nature. We see two Figures in this card, presided over by the Hierophant who is blessing them in the Sign of the Trinity.

There is yet another Path from Tiphereth to Yesod which crosses this one and influences it. This is the Path of "The Hanged Man" attributed to the Letter Mem, and the Element Water. It refers to "Writing" as the second Sepharim, and by means of Written Tradition have the true mysteries been transmitted, even thought the "writer" may never have been recognized or known to men.

Here we see a figure of a Man suspended by one foot from a gallows, his head and arms forming a triangle, above which his legs form a cross. He is the Sun of the

Sun, bringing down the Light as far as Yesod, the Subconscious Mind of Humanity. His body is reversed, as if reflected in the Waters, his Head is surrounded by Glory, the reflection of Tiphereth and Kether. His Head is thus in Yesod, the Sphere of the Moon which reflects the Sun upon the Earth, or Malkuth. The shape of the Figure in Rider's Pack perfectly symbolizes this position on the Tree.

His is the power of the Redeeming Love, usually considered as self-sacrifice, but more truly representing the Justified One, who says: "This is my body which I destroy, in order that it may be renewed." The Mysteries of the Rose Cross are transmitted through this Channel, the Initiation being attended to by "The Hierophant". Two other Paths exert their influence directly on Yesod, the Foundation, or Sphere of the Moon; one leading from Netzach, and the other from Hod. The Coils of the Twin Serpents fold back again here, the Current having absorbed the influences of the Paths of the Side Pillars through these two Sephiroth.

The Path from Netzach to Yesod continues the Influence from the Path of Leo united with that of Libra. By Tarot it is "The Chariot" which is attributed to the Sign Cancer, ruled by the Moon (Yesod). This is a very important card indeed. The Hebrew letter attributed to it is "Cheth" which is 418 the number of the Word of the Aeon ABRAHADABRA. The Charioteer is one aspect of the Lord of the Aeon, and he is in a certain sense the Initiator, for in this age the Influence of the Constellation of Taurus comes to use through the Sign Cancer according to the Precessional. He has harnessed the Black and White Sphinxes, the Traditions of Darkness and Light, and he uses them to draw his Chariot. He is under the Starry Canopy of Love. He is the Child of the Powers of the Waters, for he has descended by devious channels from the Great Sea; he is also the Lord of the Triumph of Light in its higher sense. He has the Strength of the "Lion" and the balance of "Justice" combined with the Power of Love.

Dual Moons are shown on his shoulders, for, as Cancer, he is closely connected with The Moon. The Lingam-Yoni and Winged Globe appear on his cubical Chariot which represents "The Foundation" or Yesod.

Opposite to him on the Tree is the Path from Hod to Yesod, that of "The High Priestess" or "Priestess of the Silver Star". This is attributed to "The Moon" with which Sphere it unites. This is the Channel of the Serpent of Light winding back from Hod and bringing with it the Influence of the Paths of Gemini and Virgo.

The High Priestess knows the secret powers of the "Lovers" and of the "Virgin". These she has under control in the same sense that the Charioteer controls the Sphinxes. She is truly his Counterpart. On her Lap is The book of the Law, the lost Thora of the Wheel of the Tarot, transmitted so wonderfully from the Path of IU-Pater through Chokmah, "The Sun", Tiphereth, "The Lovers", and Hod. Note that the Descent of this Law upon Tiphereth through Chokmah, was by the Paths of Kaph (20) and Resh (200) and that Liber CCXX is the Book of the Law; also that from Tiphereth, which is 6; representative of the Father 10 and the Mother 5 (as Wisdom and Understanding or IH) which make 15 and again through addition 6; it passed into the path of Zain (The Sword) 7 and to Hod 8, thus 15 = 6 and through Gimel 3 (6 + 3 = 9) to Yesod 9, where it entered the Subconscious Mind of Humanity as a seed of the Aeon.

The "Priestess of the Silver Star" is the Pure Influence of the Higher Self on the Subconscious Mind, transmitting the secret of the Star Universe and of the Silver Star. She is the Initiator into the Mysteries of Nuit, as "The Charioteer" indicates those of Hadit.

Our work, so far, has led us to an understanding of how the Universal Tradition has been imbedded in the Subconscious Mind of Humanity; built into its very Foundation and Substance. It is our Great and Glorious Heritage from the Past, made up from the Universal experience of the Race. But all men are not yet aware of this. It is still "Unconscious" in most.

Now we come to the final stages of our Journey, wherein these ideas are Manifested on the Material Plane. Malkuth, The Kingdom, is the Sphere of the Elements, and is saturated with the subtle influences, whereby the Fallen Daughter may become the Mother and bring forth Man as the Crowned Child of the Aeon.

The Path from Hod to Malkuth is by Tarot "The Magician" attributed to Mercury. This is the Wisdom and Will of the Father in Heaven brought down to the Kingdom of Earth. (Have we not prayed "Thy Will be done on Earth as it is done in Heaven" and has it not been answered "Do what thou wilt shall be the whole of the Law"). The Magician controls the Elements by means of his Four Elementary Weapons under the Direction of the Higher Will, as shown in the Card by the Wand, the Cup, the Sword, and the Pentacle. His is the Path of the Magic of Light and of Occultism. He is then the representative of the Great Father upon Earth, and his influence is within every father who realizes that he is a star.

The Path from Netzach to Malkuth is that of the "Empress" and of Venus. She represents the Love which regenerates the Kingdom when properly understood. The key shows her crowned with the Diadem of Stars. She Transmits the Understanding of the Great Mother. (So long misunderstood and thought of as the unmated and despised Woman of the Dark Sphere). Hers is the Path of Mysticism and Devotion, and of those who would be absorbed in the Absolute. She Represents the Great Mother upon Earth and is the Influence within every mother who knows Herself to be a Star.

Thus is this Kingdom supplied with Wisdom and Love, and lastly with Power, for we must finally consider the Path from Yesod to Malkuth, that of the "Pure Fool", and the All-Wandering Air, the Reconciler in all things. This is the Path of the Crowned Child of the Spirit who is in the Heart of all Humanity when he is brought to birth upon the Earth. This is the Path of those who follow neither the way of Magick nor of Mysticism, but the "Way of the Tao". These are the Masters of both Will and Love for they UNCONSCIOUSLY do the Work of the Father. Just as a Child naturally rules over his parents and is able to obtain his slightest desire, without effort, so must all Serve the Crowned Child the Lord of the Aeon.

This Path transmits the Universal Tradition of the Central Pillar-the Pillar of Mildness and Peace. This is the Pathway of the Light to be discovered amid the contending forces and the darkness of matter. This Path of the Holy Spirit of the Sun behind the Sun is that of the Letter Aleph. In it the two A's of the Beginning have become One. It is the Path of Air, the third Sepharim, or of Speech. But this is the Power of Speech in the Silence, of Harpocrates hidden within Horus. It is also the true Power, as it is written;

    Unity uttermost showed,
I adore the Might of Thy Breath,
Supreme and Terrible God
Who makest the Gods and Death
To tremble before Thee,
I, I adore Thee.

    This is the Path of IU, Horus-Harpocrates, the Ever Coming One, and of Har-Machis, Horus of the Star, the Opener of the Ways of Eternity. This is the Path of the Here and Now, transcending those of Time and Space. This is the Path of Truth, which Is Now, as It Was in the Beginning, and Ever Shall Be, MALKUTH without End. AUMN.

Chapter IV
The Sun, The Devil, and the Redeemer

One of my aims in the foregoing chapter has been to show that this is the Aeon of the Foundation of the Kingdom upon Earth, characterized by the Incarnation of God in the Heart of every Man, Woman, and Child.

It is not so much a question of "Climbing the Tree of Life" as of recognizing how all things have been working together for good so that the Source of All might become manifest in Matter, here on Earth, and the Kingdom of Ra-Hoor-Khuit be established.

We have seen in tracing out the Traditions that there have been two Wills at work, the Divine and the Personal, and that through the Ages these have appeared in conflict. One is the Bright Star or Pentagram of Unconquered Will, the other the Dark Star of the Reversed Pentagram. These two Starts are symbolized by the hands of Man, or the Magician, one raised to Heaven in the Sign of Solve, the other directed downwards in the Sign of Coagula. When united they form a Ten-fold Star, just as the hand of the man who has fallen may be grasped by the one who Raises him in the Grip of the Lion, which exactly symbolizes this uniting of the Rising and Setting Sun, or the Twins Sut-Har. For the Two Wills are Harmonized in Tiphereth.

But when we consider Malkuth, it is a question of Raising the Fallen Daughter, the Animal Soul, or Matter, to the Throne of the Mother, Understanding. That is a more difficult task, but we now have the Keys in our hands.

The Union of the two Stars as a Tenfold-Star in Malkuth is the Work before us, for this represents the Covenant God made with Abraham, as promised by the Rainbow of the old order. Having apparently lost this Symbol of the Rainbow through the alteration of the Paths, we may hope to find instead the Fulfillment of the Promise of the Covenant.

In the old order of the Paths we found Q, Sh, Th as the three influences descending upon Malkuth. QShTh is the Hebrew word for the Rainbow of Promise.

The Authority on the Qabalah, referred to in our Preface, rejected the reformulation of the paths of the Tree, partly on account of the fact of this symbolism being lost in the new arrangement. But what have we in its place? Wisdom, Love, and Power directly descending upon the Earth; the Paths of Magick and Mysticism, united by the "Way of the Tao". More than this, we have the *direct influence of the Three Supernals* upon the Kingdom. Kether, the Crown of Light, is upon the Head of the Crowned Child of the Path of Aleph, who wields the true Power of the Breath; the Wisdom of Chokmah is seen in the Path of Beth or Mercury, the Great Magician who represents the Father on Earth; while the Great Mother, Binah the Third Sephira, is translated into the Path of the Empress, the Woman of Venus, on the Path of the Mystic. So we find Father, Mother and Holy Spirit or Son, all prepared to raise the

Fallen Daughter. Yod, He, and Vau once more symbolically united with the final He. Thus the Missing members of the Body of Osiris are all brought together again; the Lost Word is recovered; the Rulers of the Four Elements of Malkuth are shown in their respective offices; and in the midst is the concealed Power of the Spirit of Shin, IU, or IO, which is 10, the number of Malkuth, as well as Kether.

The same Authority objected the some of the Alchemical Symbolism was destroyed. The Alchemists tell us that in order to make Gold, we must have Gold; and this the Gold of the Sun. What now makes Gold in our Revised arrangement? The influences descending upon Tiphereth, the Sun. We have shown how the principal Paths of Influence, which are all Solar in nature, give us 666 the Grand Number of the Sun in Tiphereth. The secondary influences are from Aries of the Golden Fleece, Scorpio the Path of "Death", or the Sun at the Dark Stage, and from Pisces which is by Tarot the "Moon". These together make the True Gold of the Sun. Again they tell us that the First Matter is the Soul of Man, and we have shown how the dual soul became divided as Adam and Eve, etc., so that you may work out this Alchemical Symbolism on other planes. But there is an even more important aspect, which this study may lead us to understand; the Inner Mystery of the Sun, the Heart of the Beast 666 which is MAN. Herein we may discover the answer to the riddle of the Sphinx, who with fixed gaze of impenetrable Mystery looks on at all the Changes of Life. Here, too, we may learn something of the Concealed Mystery of the Strange Baphomet of the ancient Templars, for all is made clear in the Reformed Order. If this is the Age of

Horus the Revealer and Opener, there is nothing hid that shall not be revealed.

Let us turn our attention for a little while to what, to some, may appear the absurd idea of The Devil. Eliphas Levi, wisely states: He who affirms the devil, creates or makes the devil. But it has elsewhere been written: Since every idea, theory or doctrine must, in the very nature of things, have some truth as its basis, it happens that the more difficult, unreasonable, or even absurd, any idea seems to be, the more illuminative does it become when thoroughly understood; for only some very important truth could have availed to give currency to a teaching of extreme incredibleness and difficulty.

Thus it is with doctrine of the devil, which, in one form or another, is found in almost every religion of the world.

The chief snare of the Devil is the Illusion of Time. Man is limited by the ideas of Time and Space, which are but modes of the human mind, as is now becoming scientifically recognized. The Black Tradition is based on Time. Saturn, the God of Time, and the Progenitor of the Devil, or Serpent of Time, is shown on the Path leading from Kether to Binah. This influence is further transmitted from Binah to Tiphereth by the Path of "The Devil" as explained before. The Hebrew letters of these Paths are Tau and Ayin, whose numerical value is 400 and 70. Ayin, Tau, or OTh is the Hebrew word for Time, or a period of Time, 470 is also the numeration of other Hebrew words meaning Eternity, or literally, a cycle of cycles. This should be sufficient evidence that the Paths are rightly placed. Taking into account the other two Paths influencing Tiphereth on this side of the Tree, which are Pe and He, or 80 and 5; we obtain

400 + 70 + 80 + 5 = 555 which is the Numeration of the Hebrew word for OBSCURITY. This certainly proves that the Dark Tradition is operative in this part of the Tree, and it accounts for much of the confusion of the "Tower" of Babel.

We have shown how the Sut-Typhonian tradition arose, so that the Son was thought to have preceded the Father, and the Mother to have been the First Cause by means of Blood. One should note in passing, that the Reciprocal Path of "The Star" is that of Aquarius which Sign governs the Blood Stream.

This tradition as far as Time is concerned led to the calculation of the Year as 365 Days, based on the Sun and Sirius Cycle. We may also notice that the Sephiroth Numbered 3, 6, and 5, are those whose influence is here depicted. They form a Triad, linked by the paths we have been discussing, and the base of this Triad is the path of "The Devil", and of the Rising Sun.

We shall have more to say in regard to the Devil, but for the moment let us turn to the other side of the Tree, and examine the Channels of the Light Tradition.

We might have done well to call these the Traditions of Black and White, for Black is that which absorbs all colors, and White that which reflects them all. The True Light is Equilibrated and Concealed in that Darkness which is higher than eyesight.

The Force of the Primum Mobile of Kether produced the Whirling motions of the "Wheel of Life" resulting in the Star Universe and Sphere of the Zodiac. Thus originated the illusion of SPACE, the other great limitation of the mind of man.

This Space became narrowed down till the idea of a Straight and Narrow Way limited all the conceptions of the followers of these Paths. The Light became but a

Twilight, and a reflection of the primal Truth, as indicated by the Path of Pisces, and the Tarot Key "The Moon". The Primal idea of the Supreme as the Concealed Life of All was soon lost. Infinite Space, filled with the Infinite but Invisible Life, became 3rd dimensional space in the minds of men. The Paths of Influence are of interest; Kaph 20, and Resh 200, give us 220, the numeration of the Book of the Law of Thelema (Will), which will eventually redeem this narrowed conception and bring back the Truth. Will is Chokmah the Sphere of Wisdom and of the Word or Logos, which was not comprehended by the Children of Darkness. This being the 2nd Sephira, makes the complete Channel from Kether to Tiphereth 222, which is the Hebrew numeration of the word for "Whiteness", thus proving our earlier speculations Qabalistically.

Taking the Sephirotic Triad as before, we find the Base is the Path of "The Sun". This in the Twilight of the Setting Sun of the White tradition, they mistook for the Lost Father, formulating the idea of ATUM-RA as the Father of the Gods. The Sun is, of course, the center of the Solar System and Ruler of the Planets; He is truly the Father of this Earth, but He is NOT THE FATHER OF THE WHOLE UNIVERSE. That is where the followers of the White Tradition made an even greater mistake than those of the Black.

The Sephiroth Tiphereth, Chokmah and Chesed, as 6, 2, 4 or 624 give us a number equivalent to the Hebrew Word for "His Covenant". The Arrow of Sagittarius (which in the old arrangement of the Paths was said to be the Arrow that pierced the Rainbow, on account of its position below Tiphereth) is seen on one of the other Paths of influence connecting this triad, and the "Moon" or "Bow" on the other. If we take these

Sephiroth in the order of 264 we get the numeration of Hebrew Words for "Footprints" literally "Foot's Breadth", and "A Straight Row" indicating the "Narrow" Way referred to before. Or as 246, we obtain "Vision" or "Aspect" denoting *Space*, as before indicated. This also seems good enough Qabalistic proof.

We may now better understand how the True Sun of a Bi-une Nature, became looked upon as SUT-HAR, and how the Traditions of the Sut-Typhonians and those of the Jupiter-Ammonians, were blended in Tiphereth.

The Influence of Har-Machis, Horus of the Star, was little understood owing to the limitations of Time and Space, though it descended as the Mediating Influence upon Tiphereth, and Welded the Twin conflicting Ideas together. The Osirians of the Right Hand Path, examining Space with great care, discovered the more correct calculation of the Year as 365 ¼ days. The Four Quarters were established, the Four Suts arose, and these were accepted as the Children of the Father Atum-Ra. Ra became the great Sun God, and the IU was lost to view in such an apparently Harmonious arrangement. So he who was the Son, became looked upon as The Father, and the Supernal Triad was no longer taken into consideration. The Pillars of the Temple of the Sun were set up. Boaz and Jachin were established in strength, as Geburah and Chesed, Severity and Mercy, and the Sun was seen between them as the Sole Lord of Light.

Followers of the old Sut-Typhonian Tradition might still secretly Symbolize Him as The Devil; followers of the Osirian Cult, as The Sun of Heaven.

Let us now return to our discussion of the Devil, or Baphomet fairly depicted, but the Symbolism of Rider's

Pack is wrong. Eliphas Levi drew him correctly, and also described him perfectly. Let me quote: "The name of the Templar Baphomet, which should be spelt Qabalistically backwards, is composed of three abbreviations: Tem., Ohp., Ab., *"Templi ominium hominum pacis abbas"*, "the father of the temple of universal peace among men." According to some, the Baphomet was a monstrous head; (Resh, the head, is the Sun); according to others, a demon in the form of a goat. (Capricorn is the Goat). A sculptured coffer was disinterred recently in the ruins of an old commandery of the temple, and antiquaries observed upon it a baphometic figure, corresponding in its attributes to the Goat of Mendes (Osiris) and the androgyne (two-sexed Horus) of Khunrath. It was a bearded figure with a female body, holding the sun in one hand and the moon in the other, attached to chains. Now this virile head is a beautiful allegory which attributes to thought alone the initiating and creating principle. Here the head represents spirit and the body matter. The orbs enchained to the human form, and directed by that nature of which intelligence is the head, are also magnificently allegorical. The sign, all the same, was discovered to be obscene and diabolical by the learned men who examined it. Can we be surprised after this at the spread of medieval superstition in our own day! One thing only surprises me, that, believing in the devil and his agents, men do not re-kindle the faggots."

The was written by Levi in 1855; even today there are many people who refuse to see the light of truth; but we are progressing.

The Figure of Baphomet, or the XVth Key of the Tarot, depicts the Symbolism of Tiphereth perfectly, from the point of view of the combined Traditions of SUT-HAR, as shown on the Revised Tree.

The Flaming Torch between the Horns is the Holy Spirit of the Path of Shin, his Horns are the Paths of SUT-HAR or of Capricorn and the Sun. The female body shows the Tradition of the Mother, while the Legs of the Goat are crossed to indicate the Passover or Crossing of the Ways after this point, as explained before. His head is that of an Ass, showing that the followers of the "Head" Doctrine of the acceptance of the Sun as the Supreme Father were foolish, but that in Tiphereth, the Heart, all things might be Harmonized. He makes the sign of Solve and Coagula, thus indicating "That which is above is like unto that which is below, and that which is below is like unto that which is above, for the performance of the Miracle of the One Substance". This is the sole Hermetic Dogma of the Microcosm and the Macrocosm; their Equivalence is found in Tiphereth. This sign also indicates the two Currents of "Will" and "will", harmonized in the Heart. This Figure should be studied with care, and it will reveal many other truths. The Caduceus in his lap, for instance, clearly shows that the Central Pillar of the Tree of Life is the Staff whereon the Twin Serpents of Time and Space are Twined.

We have explained how the Sut-Typhonians first looked upon the Great Mother as of Animal Nature, afterwards assuming her into the Heaven as the Star Goddess, Mother of the Sun. In this latter assumption they were absolutely correct, but the Worship of Nuit is practically pre-Dynastic, as is Her Symbol the Crossed Arrows. In the Darkness the idea arose of half-human, half-animal beings as representing the earliest types. The Hebrew Tradition of the First Adam corresponds to this. The Universal Tradition of the Sons of God on Earth, was lost. Man, today, is the highest of the Animals, but the lowest of the Spiritual Beings. It is the personal will and power of choice, which makes him more than animal, for he has within him a spark of the Divine Intelligence which makes it possible for him to direct his own actions, though until he discovers the Divine Will in the darkness of his own being, and aligns the personal will with It, he cannot progress. The personal will transmitted to the Heart of man from the Sphere of Geburah, is harmonized with the Divine Will of Chokmah, to the extent to which the Channels of Light are Open. But Har, the Sun of the White Tradition, was "Closer" and the True Will was little realized and understood.

We can now see that Tiphereth is a perfect Image of THE BEAST, 666, as MAN. This aspect combines in itself all that is Animal with all that is Human and all that is Spiritual and God-Like. This is the Great Solar Image which all men have worshipped and all men will worship for a long time to come. Yet it is not the Highest Truth in itself, it is a Harmonious Combination and Synthesis of Light and Darkness. Only through this Synthesis may the Truth be arrived at, however, as the Son of Man, Who was also the Son of God, has before remarked "No man cometh unto the Father but by Me". For the Son is always the visible Aspect of the Invisible and Concealed Father, who may never be known because He Is the very Essence of our Being.

The most truly representative MAN of his time is always THE BEAST, for he displays all the qualities of the Race of the Period in which he lives. We look at such a Man and see in him Ourselves, for we can only see what is within us. To some he appears an Angel of Light, to others the grinning Devil of Darkness. Thus is Genius always misunderstood and blasphemed by some, while recognized and praised by others. He is the Son, wherein Glory and Suffering are identical. He is always betrayed, always Crucified, as we see in the Path of "The Hanged Man" immediately below Tiphereth. This is the Path attributed to Water, and Water was the enemy of Horus. Why? Because his Mother was the Great Deep, and She was misunderstood and reviled as the Harlot because the true Father was invisible. Thus are Man's greatest enemies those of his own household. The Son must suffer on account of the fact that he is born of Matter, and the Soul within him is crucified, by those who see naught but Darkness, while that same Darkness conceals a Higher Light than their own.

See the proud followers of the White Tradition, whose Sun has the Head of an Ass. For Intelligence cometh from Binah the Great Mother of Understanding, and without Understanding the Way of Holiness is indeed Narrow. These are the people who are always Right, while the others are always Wrong in their sight. Their ¼ day additional in the Year makes them too proud to perceive Wider and Grander Spaces and Cycles.

But, as I hope to show, the age of narrowness is passing, and for the first time in 25,000 years, Man has the opportunity of coming into his own.

Chapter V
The Mystery of Babalon and the Beast

The Beast, or Man of the Sun, represents, as I understand it, the Soul of Humanity, or of Man, between Spirit and Matter, ashamed of neither since both are essential to His existence. The Substance of the Sun descends upon Tiphereth from Binah through the Path of "The Devil"; its Life is transmitted from Chokmah through the Path of "The Sun"; it exists as a Spiritual Idea through the Channel of "Shin" which descends from Kether. Kether is its Final and Efficient Cause, Chokmah its Formal Cause and Binah its Material Cause.

"ON" is the Ancient Egyptian Word for the Sun; as long as we are prepared to go ON, all is well since we are in line with the natural urge of Evolution. But we may rise above the ordinary idea of Evolution into a consciously free co-operation with the Divine Purpose.

The numerical value of ON is 120. This is said to have been the Age of Christian Rosencreutz at the time he passed ON.

Those who try to reverse the process of evolution, to retreat or retrogress, saying "No" in their hearts, fall into Sin which is restriction, and therefore get themselves into trouble.

ON is formed of the Hebrew Letters Ayin and Nun, thus this idea arises at the junction of the Paths of "The Devil" and "Death".

People of the "No" type arose on the other side of the Tree, on the Path of the Setting Sun. No may be spelled Nun, Vau, or NU, who was called the Father of the Waters, the reflector of Nuit.

However, we may look for a reconciliation of these ideas in the Path of "The Star" which represents the Sun at High NOON.

It was at High NOON that Parzival wrought the Miracle of Redemption, when the Spear and Cup were re-united. This Path unites the Spear of Will and Wisdom, Chokmah, with the Cup of Understanding and Intuition, Binah. The Father and Mother being thus united, the "One Star in Sight", Har-Makhu, or Horus of the Star, is recognized in His True nature as the Spirit of the Concealed Light of Kether.

The Truth was never lost to the Supernal Triad, but the Supernals were lost to the sight of man. We may wonder how this could be, and the time is now ripe for its revelation. But before an attempt is made to explain this, it is best that we should glance at the remaining Paths of the Tree, below Tiphereth.

Let us consider the Path of "The Hanged Man", sometimes called the Redeemer. Exoterically this Tarot Key is said to signify: "Enforced and not voluntary suffering"; while Esoterically it means "Self-sacrifice", but not as usually understood.

ATUM or ADAM, as the first purely Human type or Soul, is said to have been Two-sexed until he became as Adam and Eve. Tiphereth is the True Son but the false Father.

When the representative Son at this stage became mistaken for the Father, many women followed Him, seeking redemption. Thus an embarrassing situation of "enforced and not voluntary suffering" might be supposed to have arisen. The only reasonable course of action would be a concealment of the facts and a teaching which might be inferred to imply "Chastity", Celibacy, and other doctrines of repression. This is merely the exoteric view, but it accounts for the mistaken zeal of some who failed to understand the true teaching.

The Physical Sun is just as impotent to fertilize the whole Universe, although He may be entirely capable of attending to His own Solar System. He is all right in His place in the Order of the Universe; only when we misunderstand that place, do we fall into error.

The same trouble might arise in the case of a man who preached a doctrine of promiscuous sexual intercourse to a following of women; even were he a regular Lion he would be unable to supply the needs of an unlimited number and therefore be liable to attempt to retract his teaching.

The above instances could only arise on account of the lack of a true interpretation of the Word of the Justified One, Osiris arisen from Ammenti. Destruction is essential or there can be no renewal, and IU the twin-sexed supplies the answer if interpreted by means of "The Hierophant" whose Path crosses that of "The Hanged Man" and shows a reciprocal current between the Spheres of Venus and Mercury.

We have noticed how the twin-serpents "crossed over" below Tiphereth, and have studied the Symbolism rather fully. Having separated they must again re-unite in Yesod-The Foundation-and continue as One to Malkuth by the Path of Aleph, the Pure Fool.

We may now consider Malkuth, the Fallen Daughter, who, according to the Qabalah, in order to be redeemed must Unite with the Son, be raised to the Throne of the Mother, re-awaken the Father so that all things are re-absorbed into the Crown.

This process has been much misunderstood, it has been thought to imply a *return* to the Crown. The Mystics have all wanted to be re-absorbed into the Absolute. The Magicians, on the other hand, have tended to keep going ON, and to attempt to usurp the Throne of God, which rightfully belongs to the Mother.

Both met with a terrible Abyss, while working on the old methods.

The Magician traveled up the "Tree" till he came to Chesed as an Exempt Adept who had built up a wonderful system of knowledge, only to find the whole structure must be broken in pieces in the Abyss, if he hoped to Attain to true Understanding and Wisdom. Few passed this Ordeal.

The Mystics, on the other hand, being of the negative type, opened their minds and souls to the "light" and often mistook false lights for the True One. Having a very limited basis of experience as a foundation of their Pyramid, the Apex was proportionately low, and the Light they saw at that point, they attributed to their own pet divinity as their savior and redeemer. The Dawning of Solar Consciousness (Dhyana) tended to come as such a shock that most of these Mystics lost their balance for a time, if not for the remainder of their incarnation. If they went further, they were literally flooded with the Dark Forces of the Abyss. Some of these truly saw the Devil, and believed in him, and preached his existence to their followers. They certainly never say God.

Many of these people lived a very holy and chaste life, according to the standards of their time, before reaching this stage. Afterwards, the ignorant believed in them as men of good reputation, and were even content to "believe" without further desire for actual experience.

So we find a line of "Theorists" arose, under the guidance of "Partly Disillusioned" people who feared to go further and so taught a doctrine of Fear which is the forerunner of Failure, a doctrine of implicit belief in the leader of the movement, amounting in some cases to a "blind faith" in Substitutes, Reflections, Vicarious Atonement, and anything else but the necessity of working out their own Salvation. Yet there is an element of truth even in such apparently absurd notions as Vicarious Atonement; just as we found an element of truth in the doctrine of the Devil. Every man and every woman who Attains, make it just that much easier for the rest of Humanity to reach perfection. The whole Race must eventually Attain, for it is bound together by the closest ties, so that the process cannot be finally complete in the individual until the Last has become as the First in the Kingdom of Heaven upon Earth.

We seem far from that issue, but the Way is now OPEN, as before it was Closed, for Horus the Opener has taken his Seat in the East at the Equinox of the Gods.

But, to return to Earth, or Malkuth, as the Fallen Daughter. The true teaching, as I see it, is this. Malkuth, the Sphere of the Elements, or Matter, has been mistaken for the Planet Earth in place of *All the Material Substance of the Universe in manifested form*. Matter, as we should know, is *continuous*.

The Sun is the God of this world, its Physical Father, and as such he is worthy of our utmost respect and reverence. We do well to salute and recognize Him as Ra in the four Quarters. We "see" Him in the Rising, the Midday, and the Setting Sun; we "believe" in Him as the Sun of Midnight, our "heads" tell us that He is Osiris of the Underworld.

These are the old doctrines of the "Eye" and the "Head" transmitted to our subconscious minds from the Paths of "Ayin" and "Resh". "Seeing is believing", is a saying that held sway until the Scientists showed us we could not believe in the testimony of our senses. But the whole doctrine of the Birth, Death and Resurrection of the Sun or Son, was based on this dogma.

Also, just as of old the Sut-Typhonians tradition became despised, so Woman has been despised and held down by Man, by the son who had usurped the place of the Father. In this Man is truly a beast, and it required a Greater Beast, a practical living example, to show him his error, folly and wrong-doing. But man misunderstands and fears the Beast, who after all offers him the Secret of the Solar Pathway to the Stars. Why does he fear? The old Dark Tradition in his subconscious mind, holds him back. He fears to enter the Darkness of Night, lest he lose what little light he has therein. But this is the result of his limited earth-bound conception, which is quite un-scientific and gross.

If we truly believe in Osiris (or Christ) why should we fear to descend with Him into the Underworld? Jesus is said to have done so, before he rose again in Spirit to His Father in Heaven, thus uniting His True Self with the Invisible Central Star of the Universe.

Day and Night only exist for us on this Planet; the Sun does not travel round the Earth for our convenience. We, on this Planet, travel round the Sun, revolving as we go. Thus his Light only reaches certain parts of the Earth at any one time, and the rest of the Planet is in darkness. The Sun is always Shining, and if we come to consider things from the point of view of the Sun, we shall begin to shine too.

But the Sun, although Father of this Planet, is but the Son of the Great Mother, the Star Universe. Where then is the True Father? This is the question that puzzled the old Sut-Typhonians in the earliest times. The difficulty arose through the original Illusions of Time and Space, which have kept the World in ignorance since the last Golden Age. The Universe is Infinite in the Here, but men have tried to circumscribe it. The Infinite is ever present in the Now, but Men have looked backwards and forwards as if time were a line. There are Two Infinites, or conceptions of the Infinite, the Infinitely Great and the Infinitely Small. The extent of the One escapes us, the Present Moment of Pure Being escapes us. The Infinitely Great, is Nuit, Continuous Matter, Mother of the Stars. The Infinitely Small and un-extended point, is Hadit, the Inmost Essential Self of All, the Flame that burns in every heart of man and in the core of every Star. Both these are invisible to our Senses and Minds.

Since these are the Infinite, the Center is Everywhere and the Circumference Nowhere. Every point in Space is equally the Center of the Whole, there being no Limit. The True Father is Invisible, but the Center of all. Men called him "Father Time" but he is Father "Now." The Now became extended as the Serpent of Time, Saturn, who tempted Eve, Matter, and caused the Fall but Now is the accepted Time, Now is the Day of Salvation. The Illusion of Space, on the other hand, made it difficult to imagine or find the Center; study the Stars as we would. Imagining a possible Limit, men failed to perceive how that Center could be everywhere present at the same moment of Time.

The Long Lost Father, Hadit, is the true Life of All, and the Eternal Energy of All. Matter and Energy can never be separated, one always merges into the other in a continuous and continual Marriage Union. The Universe, as we know it, or may come to know it through Spiritual Perception, is the Result of that Union, the Crowned Child in the fullest sense.

Men and women of this Planet may think of the Secret Father as the Sun, till they draw that Sun within the Heart, and look at things from His viewpoint. This is the Balanced and Harmonious conception of the Great Beast which is MAN. Then we realize that the whole Solar System revolves around Its Central Sun, and so on to Infinity. There is No Limit to the Expansion of Consciousness in the Here and Now, for Hadit, the true Father is Now in each one of us, veiled by the Light of the Sun of our being, His Manifest Son of Light. Truly the Kingdom of Heaven is within us, it will never be found outside amid the illusions of space and time. Those who have sought the Kingdom of Heaven within, have rejoiced therein; but that is an experience each must Attain for himself by Work. Let us then return to the general discussion of the subject.

We have said that Malkuth was mistaken for the Planet Earth, which she only is in a narrow sense. If united with the Son, or Sun, she begins to view the universe from His standpoint. Around her revolve the planets of the Solar System, of which Earth is one of the smallest. But it is said she must be raised to the Throne of the Mother from which she fell. She must be understood as the Original Substance, or pre-elemental matter. Also her throne is the Sphere of Saturn, the outermost of the (then known) planets. On reaching Solar Consciousness she must not imagine that she has arrived at the Goal. This is the mistake made by those who are obsessed by the results of Dhyana, the earliest Illumination. She must *expand* to the Rim of the Wheel, the Orbit of Saturn. She will gaze at the Great Zodiac, the Star Universe in Chokmah. She will seek to absorb this as the Father, her True Mate, and in so doing will Expand to Infinity as Nuit, The Ain, finding Kether, the True Father of Her Being, or Hadit, at Her Center, made Visible by the Extended Light of the Ain Soph Aur, which is Ra-Hoor-Khuit, the Lord of the Aeon. Having been assumed unto Heaven her effort will be to Contract upon the Center, and to Bring forth the Child. But she is Virgin, and the child is not born but "Ever Coming." The Force and Fire of the Universe ever Expands within Her. Thus we may conceive of the Two Infinites multiplied in the Crowned Child.

All these Mysteries may be discerned Spiritually by the Children of Earth who have within them the Light of the Crown. Man, the Microcosm, the Little Universe, is like unto God the Macrocosm. This is the great Mystery. The Soul, Malkuth, is capable of taking into itself, Spiritually, all that is in the Macrocosm, until able to think the One Thought of God, which is the Universe itself.

The Animal Soul is that which perceives and feels, without it we may not perceive or feel the Joys of the Universe. Despised as the Fallen Daughter, it is our greatest Treasure, for it is The Kingdom of Heaven upon Earth. We may now understand the Mystery of Revelation, of the Woman Clothed with the Sun, becoming great with Child. How the Beast, tried to Devour the Child, and stop further progress, in order that he might continue to be Worshipped as the Lord of Heaven. How the Woman escaped into Egypt, or expanded to the limits of the Mother of Sut, the Orbit of Saturn and so on till the True Child was brought to Light *within* Her and the light of the Sun and Moon were no longer needed, for there was the Crowned Child in the Midst of the Holy City.

So we may learn, through the expansion of our consciousness to the conception of Babalon and the Beast, to pass ON to the Greater Conception of Nuit and Hadit, and obtain our heritage of Cosmic Consciousness, as the Crowned Children of the New Aeon. This was prophesied by the Beast Himself, who made it his life work to teach; "First obtain the Knowledge and Conversation of the Holy Guardian Angel, the Higher Self, in Tiphereth the Kingdom of God in the Heart, and all things shall be added unto you."

Is it not written in the Qabalah: "Kether is in Malkuth, and Malkuth is in Kether, but after another manner"? This statement has been misunderstood owing to the limitations of our minds. Malkuth is NUIT, and Kether is HADIT, and when united RA-HOOR-KHUIT, their Son is in Tiphereth. Also Nuit has said "My number is Eleven, as are all their numbers who are of us." Kether is 1, Malkuth is 10, together Eleven, which is the Lost Sphere of DAATH, the Child of Chokmah and Binah. This is the Mystery of the Path of Aquarius, The Star, the Eleventh Sign of the Zodiac, brought to Earth at the Eleventh Hour, before Time had swallowed the Last of His Children, which shall be as The First in the Kingdom of the Here and Now.

Chapter VI
Further Light on the Tree of Life

We should now try to understand the Mystery of "The Tree of Life which is one with the Tree of Knowledge." It is written: "The letter killeth and the Spirit giveth life."

The Structure of the Tree of Life as represented in our diagram is evidently a Divinely given Plan of the Multi-dimensional Sphere of the Universe, in Two-Dimensions. When we examine it superficially it means little or nothing; gradually, as we absorb the Divine Ideas reflected through its medium, our minds take on the Image and Likeness of God, and we are enabled to comprehend all in Spherical form.

The Qabalah teaches us to think of a greater and greater number of things, in the light of fewer and fewer Ultimate Ideas, as has been shown in the chapter on "The Essence of the Practical Qabalah." The highest Reason which is in God and which is God, is absolutely

One. God knows all things by One Idea, which is identical with His Being.

The limitations of Time and Circumstance obsess us, and we are at first unable to grasp the Divine Plan. Tradition is the result of the Thought of Humanity in the "past" focused in the Present, the Here and Now. So it is in regard to what we term the "future." The Plan of the Tree of Life gives us an idea of the Unchanging Basis of the Here and Now, in time and space.

The Reformulation of the Paths has made this clear; we have seen how the past leads to the Present, and glimpsed a Vision of the Great Light of the Beginning, which will Dawn on Humanity in the "future." Those who are able to comprehend may obtain this Reward Now. Nuit has said: "I give unimaginable joys on *earth*, certainty, not faith, while in life upon death, peace unalterable, rest, ecstasy, nor do I demand aught in sacrifice." Or as Christ said to one of the two thieves (Time and Space), "This Day shalt thou be with me in Paradise"; and on another occasion; "Now is the Accepted Time, Now is the Day of Salvation."

Let us examine the Tree of Life again in order that we may further grasp its mystery, and how it comes about that the New Aeon is possible in Human Consciousness. We must use the language of time and space, but we shall be informed of the Spirit if our minds are open to the Truth.

Horus, the Ever-Coming Son, is said to have appeared under many forms, as the Great Cycle of the Precession of the Equinoxes progressed. The Complete Cycle is said to be 25868 years; though in more ancient reckoning it was 26000 years, when the year was taken to represent 360 days. 2155 Years represents one Sign on the Grand Zodiac, and every 2155 years Horus appears in a new guise. About 11,030 B.C. He would have appeared in the Sign of Leo, as the Lion God. If we examine the position of this Path on the Tree, we find it unites Tiphereth and Netzach. It is my opinion that the consciousness of Humanity during that period would be particularly influenced by that Path, and that the flower of the race could not have held conceptions above Tiphereth. They may have obtained a glimpse of the Sun as Ruler of the Elements. About 8875 B.C., Horus would be manifest through Cancer, as the Beetle, and the summit of Human consciousness would be lowered. Thus the age would seem one of retrogression, until Horus, dipping down into Yesod, re-ascended under the Moon's Influence thus entering Gemini. This seems indicated in the Tarot Trump "The Moon" where we notice the Beetle coming up from the Pool beneath the Moon. About 6720 B.C. He entered Gemini and appeared as one of the Twins. Consciousness would balance that of the Leo period, and tend to ascend to Tiphereth. In 4565 B.C. Horus entered Taurus, appearing as a Calf. Moses seemed to consider the worship of the Calf a retrogression, and we see that the Path of Taurus is again below Tiphereth. In 2410 B.C. we find Him appearing in Aries, as the Lamb. This represented a distinct rise in the Race Consciousness, which however took on the Strong but Severe aspect of Geburah. This period was a Natural One, for the Constellation Aries, would coincide with the Sign of Aries in the Earth's Aura or Elliptic. This conflicting Time Cycles would be reconciled. Then, in 255 B.C. we find him as the Fish, the Path balancing that of Aries, and having the Influence of Mercy predominating. Thus it was till 1900 A.D. when He appeared to enter

Aquarius. But what a startling change. Suddenly we find Him on a Path uniting the Supernals of Wisdom and Understanding, and Their direct Influence made possible in the Minds of the Race. Not since the previous Golden Age 25000 years ago had the Influence of this Path been felt. No wonder men looked to the Sun as the Father, and even in the Pisces period only understood the lower Aspect of Jupiter. Once again in this Aeon we are able to recognize the Great Mother of the Stars, and to discover the Secret of the Lost Father.

There is also a Trinitarian Cycle of Father, Mother, Child, running parallel, so to speak, with this Tradition of the Evercoming Horus. It is the Natural Formula of Isis, Osiris, Horus, and is of Solar Origin. From 2419 B.C. to 255 B.C. Isis the Mother was said to be the Predominant Aspect of the Trinity. Hers was the Office of Nature, She presided over the Natural opening of the Great and Little Years which both coincided. Then Osiris, Dead and Re-Arisen, was the predominant object of Worship till 1900 A.D., and self-sacrifice and Renunciation were the principal exoteric formulae. In this present Cycle Horus is doubly pre-dominant, so we see Him in his Dual Nature as Horus-Harpocrates.

It is also interesting to note the character of Horus as Apophis the Avenger. The Isis, Osiris, Horus arrangement is quite the natural one for the course of events. Isis (The Moon) having taken the place of the Great Mother Nuit. But what of the Formula IAO, as Isis, Apophis, Osiris? If we make a list of several repetitions of the series thus:

Isis
Osiris
Horus
Isis

Osiris
Horus
Isis
etc.

and trace them back, we find the order Isis, Horus, Osiris, etc.; or Isis, Apophis, Osiris. Horus appears as the avenger Apophis to those who try to GO BACK, or retrogress. He has to destroy them in order that they may be renewed. But as long as we go forward, we travel with the Ever Coming Son, who is after all our Destiny, since He is within each of us as the True Urge of our Being. This, then, is the secret of the Way of the TAO; step boldly out on the Path of Destiny, having aligned the personal with the Divine Will, and thus prepared oneselves for the acceptance of that Destiny. Keep ahead of the urge from behind, and it will not fret us.

Then we become Free, Goers, Doing the Will of God upon Earth, Ever-Coming Sons of God.

But if we attempt to lag behind to carry out some personal whims and wishes, Destiny catches up with us and forces us on. To those who willfully turn back and seek to avoid cooperating with the Divine Plan, Horus is the Great Avenger. Has he not said "I am a God of War and of Vengeance. I will deal hardly with them."

Thus at his Coming in 1904 he found the Race in a state of definite retrogression. "Civilization" met him as he advanced in triumph, and millions fell, without understanding what was happening. He still drives ahead in His Chariot, and millions more will feel his Force and Fire, until the Race recognizes that it must right about face, and cheer the Conquering Hero on. Then we shall have Peace and Rejoicing, and the Stern Warrior will seem as the Gentlest Child.

Chapter VII
The Law of Thelema

To some, this book will come in the nature of a challenge, to others as the fulfillment of the Covenant symbolized by the Rainbow of Hope. Some will understand readily, some will desire to understand and seek further enlightenment, others will partly understand and try to forget what they have read, some may definitely disagree. But one thing is certain "The sin which is unpardonable is knowingly and willfully to reject truth, to fear knowledge lest that knowledge pander not to thy prejudices."

I have tried to avoid the unpardonable sin by keeping an open mind for all that seemed to express an aspect of truth, even where I failed to understand the full significance of the teaching.

Take, for instance, the statement of the Master Therion "Do what thou wilt shall be the whole of the Law," which has been much misunderstood by some people.

When I first heard this statement, many years ago, it shocked and surprised me; it did not seem possible that such a doctrine could be of universal application. But I did not reject it on that account.

When I read the "Message of the Master Therion," I found it clearly stated and explained that "Do what thou wilt" does not mean "Do what you like." What then does it mean? That I have tried to discover, by means of experiment, and I have found, as stated by Therion, that far from leading to "license" it becomes the "strictest possible bond."

One can hardly fail to realize that we have been living in an age of "restriction" which has led to most direful results. But the solution of the difficulty is evidently not to be found in a mad breaking away from all authority and order, a running wild with cries of "freedom" and "liberty" only to find ourselves more enslaved than before. What then is the solution of the difficulty? I will endeavor to tell you how this teaching has worked out in practice in my life and consciousness.

I considered the matter seriously and said "If do what thou wilt shall be the *whole* of the Law" it evidently applies to all mankind. In that case my own personal will is but a little part of the will of Humanity, and in doing it I must learn first of all to consider other people's wills more than anything else. If all the people come to do their wills, what is left to be done must be my will, and my course become clear. Therefore let me learn to mind my own business, cease to make any attempt to interfere with the will of another, and see what results.

I found, as soon as I was less anxious to tell everyone else just what, in my opinion, they should do,

I gained many true and devoted friends, who have never since deserted me, except through the change called death. People seemed to feel that I had no personal axe to grind, and gave me their brotherly and sisterly confidence. I, at the same time, found there was a great deal it was my will to do, which no one else seemed interest in undertaking, so that I continued very happily doing what I felt to be right, without coming into serious conflict with anyone. I did not feel that my will was in opposition to the laws of the Country, or the City, and so these in no way restricted me in a personal sense. I began to feel this was one of the chief rules of life, a good common-sense business proposition. It seemed so plain that I almost wondered why people had not adopted it before. Then I began to notice its effects on others who were also endeavoring to live it. In some cases their interpretation at first seemed to be "Do your will regardless of the other fellow," but they very soon found this did not work at all in their dealings with me, at any rate. If such came along and made a rough demand, or a stupid statement of what he would, or would not do to me, I simply said "Go ahead and do it but don't expect me to help you." The result was in every instance, since there was no opposition and I didn't really care one bit, that his ardor cooled and he changed his mind; some better way having occurred to him at once. Opposition and resistance in such cases would have been just the same as helping the other person to fulfill what was quite evidently a hasty choice of action, and had I followed that course, I should not alone have done something I did not feel to be right, but have aided him to do something he would afterwards have found to be wrong, and we might both have bitterly regretted the transaction.

I began to realize that the True Will of Humanity as a Whole was the same as the Will of God for Humanity at this particular stage of their development. Therefore by trying to help Humanity as a Whole, without distinction, as far as in me lay, I could learn to do the Will of God, or the True Will. I found this entirely satisfied my "personal will" for I realized that I was living for a greater purpose than I could personally formulate as a plan of action by means of the little "will." Herein then lay the secret of "Do what thou wilt shall be the whole of the Law," it was a divinely sent promise to encourage Humanity in its Hour of Darkness.

The more I endeavored to live up to this Law, the easier I found it became. It is very nearly the same as the Law of least resistance, for one takes advantage of the Inertia of the Universe.

There could be no turning aside, it became a Conscious and Free fulfillment of Destiny, a co-operation in the plan of the Great Architect. This Plan became clearer and clearer. Problems that had perplexed me for years, gradually solved themselves, without effort on my part. Things I had tried hard to do, by means of the personal will alone, became easy. I obtained all the personal pleasure of the fulfillment, without the effort to attain them. I learned to tackle each problem at the time it arose, and to clear it up while it was small. My "duty" became plain, and it was my Will to do it while I had the opportunity. I found I had just enough work to do properly, without time to spare to do anything for others they could better do for themselves; but there was always enough time to help another on a point I could obviously clear up, and on which he really needed my help.

I began to notice calls on my attention from "outside" and to give them prior consideration. That is to say, if something "came to me to do" I tried to do it with my might; but I curbed, as far as possible the tendency to "look for trouble" that would not otherwise come my way. Thus I am finding "Do what thou wilt" is helping me to find *my particular place* in the scheme of things. I am beginning to like all I do, which is much more satisfactory that trying to "do what I like."

This book is one of the results of my course of action. I spent many years as an Accountant, which work I did without it being particularly congenial to me. I found it became possible for me to make a living in more congenial ways, so that I became happier, if not so well off financially, than I had been. At the same time I feel that the result of my researches, which have given me great pleasure and keen enjoyment, may be of real service to those whose work does not permit them to apply the same amount of time to preparation and study that I have been able to devote to it. More of my brothers and sisters may therefore profit by my work, than would have been the case had I continued with my profession as an accountant.

In the light of this book, in which, I hope, shines a glimmering of the Universal Tradition, the statement "Do what thou wilt shall be the whole of the Law" will be even plainer to humanity. It is literally the TOUCHSTONE of our lives. This one thing which makes Man more than animal is the power of will or choices of action; the power of Intelligent Purpose. The Black Tradition interpreted this power wrongly, and thought by "personal will" to usurp the Power of God. God was Invisible to them, they could see no reason why they should not do anything they liked, regardless of the other fellow, so long as they had the power or the money to carry out their ambition. The White Brotherhood, while receiving the Will of God, allowed their Interpretation of that Will to become so narrow, that they felt themselves alone to be Right and all others Wrong. Such are the reformers, however well-meaning. But the Universe is the Perfect Work of a Perfect Being. If we see wrong in it, it is owning to our own limited outlook.

THELEMA, or "Do what thou wilt," is a TOUCHSTONE in this respect. If we accept it and interpret it to mean the doing of the "personal will" only, we find Destiny steps in and stops us. If we still persist, willfully going against the Divine Will, against what is for the Good of Humanity as a Whole, against the Natural Urge of Evolution; trying to interfere with the will of others, and to usurp the Divine Right of every man and every woman to be THEMSELVES; we meet Horus the Avenger, and are deservedly smashed out of all recognition, ready to be made over again some other time when Nature has nothing better to do.

If we grudgingly submit to Fate and allow ourselves to be slowly pushed along by the Evolutionary process, we cannot expect much comfort or success. We are practically slaves, little better than animals.

If, on the other hand, we accept Divine Law, search our Hearts in the effort at all times to discover the Will of God within us, and to put our personal will in line with the Divine; we shall become Men and Women with a True Purpose. We shall step on the Road of Destiny, which is one with Free-will so long as it be

God's Will, with a certainty and Courage which will be a living example and help to all around us. We cannot teach better than by example. Let us then seek constantly to do the Will of God which is our own True will, and we shall soon realize "There is no law beyond: Do what thou wilt!"

Chapter VIII
The Tradition of the Golden Age

A great deal more might be said on this subject, in fact it is truly inexhaustible, for fresh Light is Ever Coming.

There are one or two points which seem of particular interest and importance, and these I should Like to mention in the present treatise, so as to make is as complete and comprehensive as possible, as far as it goes.

I feel I have submitted fairly substantial evidence in justification of the Reformulation of the Order of the Paths, but I may point to some other interesting facts.

Firstly, the Path from Malkuth to Yesod is Aleph. Above Yesod and below Tiphereth we find the Paths of Vau and Mem, forming a Cross. These together are AUM, the word whereby we may prolong Dhyana, etc. But since M, the last letter is a closed sound and represents Death, we have been using the Word AUMN for some time, as this prolongs the Breath through the nasal sound of N, thus showing that Death may be overcome. We find the Path of Nun, N, or "Death" immediately above Tiphereth; so by this means we may be said to pass ON. This formula brings us directly in contact with the Channel of the Holy Spirit, or Shin.

I may say a new Ritual was revealed to us early this Year. I do not intend to describe it on account of its great Power. It might be a hindrance rather than a help to those unprepared for it. All I shall say is, that what we may term the 1923 Qabalistic Cross has the effect of Enlightening the Subconscious Mind by means of Wisdom and Understanding, thus enabling us, while on Earth, to ascend through the Power of the Breath, overcoming Water and Fire in the Light of the Spirit. Those who are ready will understand without further explanation. The Ascending Sign is that of Apophis as the Triple Flame.

While mentioning formulae we might also point out an exact correspondence to that of the Ritual of Mercury as indicated in the present arrangement of Paths. Taht, or Mercury, assisted Horus, be it remembered, in his struggle against the Powers of the Waters, by means of his Knowledge of the luni-solar reckonings. The Ritual states "The Sun is thy Father, thy Mother the Moon, the Wind hath borne thee in its bosom, and Earth hath ever nourished the changeless Godhead of thy Youth." In other words: The Sun (Tiphereth) is thy Father; thy Mother (Mem) the Moon (Yesod); the Wind (Aleph) hath borne thee in its bosom; and Earth (Malkuth) hath ever nourished the Changeless Godhead (Hadit) of the Youth (IU).

Now let us discuss a slightly different aspect. The Root of the word Qabalah is QBL, meaning "to receive." The Numeration of QBL is 132 which suggests the Supernal Triad. The word Qabalah is in Hebrew QBLH. The Final He suggests the Daughter, Malkuth. Kether,

Chokmah, Binah, are the Sephirotic Roots of the Elements Air, Fire, and Water. Malkuth alone is attributed to Earth which is a compound of the other three. Therefore QBLH implies that Malkuth is "To Receive" the "Roots" of the Primordial Elements directly from the Supernals, and is composed thereof.

It has been shown how the Path of "The Magician" is directly representative of the Will and Wisdom of the Father in Chokmah, or of Yod of Tetragrammaton. Also how the Path of "The Empress" is directly representative of the Understanding of the Great Mother Binah, or of the He of IHVH. Again how the Path of "The Fool" transmits the Power of Vau, the Son, and of the Spirit or Shin. We find all these within the Daughter or final He, which becomes one with IHShVH, which, as 326, has also been shown to be the numeration of PARChVAL the earliest spelling of the Fool which is Aleph, the One who is in All. 326 is also indicated in the Descending Triad of Binah, Chokmah, Tiphereth; symbolizing that Tiphereth is also within Malkuth in the Complete Sphere, of which Malkuth or Nuit is the Infinite Circumference, Kether the Invisible and Infinitely Small Center, or Hadit; while Tiphereth, as Ra-Hoor-Khuit, is the Finite Universe, capable of being absorbed into the Heart or Soul of Man, half-way, so to speak, between the Infinites. The Sphere of the Moon, Yesod, is the Subconscious Mind of Humanity which absorbs the Solar Seed of Truth, and reflects it to the Individual Soul.

This can be shown in another manner. If we take Malkuth as the Planet Earth, the Air (Aleph) circles around it. Then comes the Orbit of the Moon. We may imagine Yesod circling round Malkuth with her reflecting surface always toward it. This orbit of the

Moon may be fittingly taken for the Aura of the Earth, capable of receiving every impression and transmitting it to the Subconscious.

Malkuth and its Moon travel round the Sun, Tiphereth, and the elliptic is the Aura of the Earth in a larger sense; since the Signs of the Zodiac retain a fixed relation to the Earth as imaginary divisions of this elliptic, even though the actual constellations have changed their positions owing to the precession of the Equinoxes. This causes the actual Constellation to extend its influence through a different Sign. For instance, at present (since 1900), the Constellation of Aquarius exerts its influence upon the Sun, through the Sign of Aries, and this influence is transmitted to the Earth.

This Orbit of the Earth, is however a part of the Aura of the Sun, which may be said to extend to the Orbit of Saturn. (More properly Neptune in the light of modern discovery.)

Between the Earth and the Sun, as we look to Him as a Center, revolve the Planets Mercury and Venus. If, therefore, we Worshipped the Sun as our main objective, we should find ourselves traveling to a false Center. So we must turn our backs to the Sun, looking at things from His point of view, while still on the Earth, and around us will appear the Orbits of Mars, then Jupiter and then of Saturn, outside which are the Constellations of the Zodiac, and so on. From this symbolical viewpoint we may begin to absorb all these within us, as before stated in a slightly different way.

Now the Sun is ever the Son of the Star Mother, but as Father of Earth He transmits the prevailing influence of the Starts to the Earth through the medium of the Moon's orbit. If, from Earth, we look up at the Sun at the Vernal Equinox, which opens the Year, we should see him with the first Degrees of the Constellation Aquarius as a background. The Sun's Aura is particularly affected by the Influence of this Constellation, during the 2155 Years it appears back of the Zodiacal Sign of Aries in the Earth elliptic. The Life-force from the Sun is therefore charged with this Influence, and all on Earth are accordingly affected.

The Breath, or Prana, of the Sun is transmuted in the Body of Man, and he tends to become the Type of the Aquarian Age. This is a purely Human Sign, of the Water-bearer who carries the Waters of Life fearlessly. Horus has overcome the terror of the Waters, his ancient enemy, and to him that overcometh shall be given of the Waters of Life freely.

One could draw many parallels from the Scriptures to show that this is the Age of Fulfillment; even the FULL-FILLING of MAN with the Water of Life. Readers may, however, be interested in tracing some of these for themselves in "Revelations" and elsewhere.

We should remember, however, that Horus is the Ever-coming Son. This is not merely His second coming, any more than the last manifestation was His first.

At the risk of repeating myself I want to point out once again, from the Tree of Life, what a very important Age we have entered. In the last period, the influence of the Path of Pisces being predominant, it was next to impossible to rise above the Sphere of Chesed. Jupiter was the Highest conception of the Father known to man. It was an age of Mercy, unbalanced, and tending to aid and abet evil, just as the period before that was Over-severe and cruel. Without tracing all these paths again, let me once more say that the Path of Aquarius (if our plan is accepted as the correct one) is the ONLY Path of a Reciprocal nature among the Supernals, and the only Zodiacal Path above the Abyss. Therefore the coming period of 2132 years, is the ONLY period in the Cycle of 25000 years, when Humanity has the advantage of the True Light of Wisdom and Understanding. At the end of this period, we may expect another FALL, just as Lucifer Fell at one period, and Eve at another. Then the Influence will be in the Path of Capricorn, or "The Devil," and the Light will decline towards Tiphereth as the principal manifestation of God according to the "Eye" Doctrine.

We may now understand why it was that the Ancient Brethren of the previous Golden Ages, seeing all things clearly, and realizing the future as well as the past, made very effort to leave PERMANENT MEMORIALS and LANDMARKS for the guidance of Humanity who would arise during the twilight and dark periods that must inevitably follow HIGH NOON. Our endeavor during this cycle should be to leave just such a permanent record, in Living form if possible. The formation of the Twelve Tribes as Living representatives of the Signs of the Zodiac was just such an attempt in the past. The Jews were the IUs, representatives of the Ever-coming Son, the Wanderer, and thus they were called the chosen people. They were the people to which IUsaas came, hoping to find they still had a recollection of the Universal Tradition. But they had lost it, and did not understand. So He had to be content with promising the Gentiles that He would Come Again, and that next time it would be at the Eleventh Hours, in the Sign of Aquarius, and that the Golden Age would be renewed for a period. "In my

Father's House are many mansions," He said, "I go to prepare a place for you." In other words, "This limited and restricted Sign of Pisces is which I am now appearing, leaves much to be desired." He knew He must be misunderstood, that the IUs having failed Him there was no chance of reviving the Lost Tradition, that the World would have to fulfill its destiny. He tried to explain to a few disciples, making each of the represent one of the Signs, so as to form a new Circle corresponding to the Tribes. Most of these have misunderstood, as time has shown.

Now He comes as a Conqueror, not as a Slave; but his chief weapon will be His Childlike Simplicity and His failure to perceive anything but good in all around him. For He knows that the Universe is the Perfect Work of a Perfect Being, that Existence is pure Joy, that the sorrows are but shadows, they pass and are done, but there is that which remains.

Now, in conclusion, let us say a few words in regard to Hermes, He who has given us His Book, the Tarot, as a true token of remembrance, of Whom we have one indisputably authentic record in the famous Emerald Tablet; all that is left of the Wisdom of Hermetic Philosophy of Ancient Egypt. Hermes prophesied that Egypt would fall, and so She did. He say there would come an end to the Golden Age in which He lived.

What says the Emerald Tablet. "True, without error, certain and most true; that which is above is as that which is below, and that which is below is as that which is above, for the performing of the miracle of the One Thing (or One Substance); and as all things were from one, by the mediation of one, so all things arose from this one thing by adaptation; the father of it is the Sun, the mother of it is the Moon; the wind carries it in its belly; the nurse thereof is the Earth. This is the father of all perfection, or consummation of the whole world. The power of it is integral, if it be turned into earth. Thou shalt separate the earth from the fire, the subtle from the gross, gently with much sagacity; it ascends from the earth to heaven, and again descends to earth; and receives the strength of the superiors and of the inferiors-so thou hast the glory of the whole world; therefore let all obscurity flee before thee. This is the strong fortitude of all fortitudes, overcoming every subtle and penetrating every solid thing. So the world was created. Hence were all wonderful adaptations of which this is the manner. Therefore am I called Thrice Great Hermes, having the Three Parts of the philosophy of the whole world. That which I have written is consummated concerning the operation of the Sun."

May Hermes, Thrice Greatest, guide the earnest seeker in his study of this book. May He enlighten the minds of those who study the Emerald Tablet, comparing it with the teaching herein set forth, the Keys of the Tarot, and the Reformulation of the Paths. It is enough if I add that the Three Parts of the philosophy of the whole world, the Three Supernals, now directly exert their Influence upon the Earth, through the Channels of Wisdom, Love and Power, and that in very Truth "That which is above is as that which is below, and that which is below is as that which is above, for the performing of the miracle of the One Thing" which One Thing is the One Thought of the Supreme and Concealed Father, as Manifested in the Ever-Coming Son.

Made in the USA
Las Vegas, NV
08 May 2024